THE UPSIDE-DOWN CHURCH

THE
UPSIDE DOWN CHURCH

GREG LAURIE

WITH
DAVID KOPP

Tyndale House Publishers, Inc.
WHEATON, ILLINOIS

Visit Tyndale's exciting Web site at www.tyndale.com

Edited by Vinita Hampton Wright

Book jacket design by David Riley+Associates, Corona Del Mar, CA

Library of Congress Cataloging-in-Publication Data

Laurie, Greg.
  The upside-down church / Greg Laurie.
      p.   cm.
  ISBN 0-8423-7812-X (hc : alk. paper)
  ISBN 0-8423-7847-2 (sc : alk. paper)
  1. Church growth.   I. Title.
BV652.25.L38   1999
254′.5—dc21   98-51016

Printed in the United States of America

05   04   03   02   01   00
7   6   5   4   3   2   1

CONTENTS

THE UPSIDE-DOWN CHURCH

God's Original Plan Was the Right One

I SUPPOSE I should be the last person writing a book on what a church ought to be. I have been a Christian only since 1970. I was not raised in the church. In fact, I had no background whatsoever in an understanding of the evangelical culture. I was your garden variety unbeliever. It's not that I was *somewhat* ignorant of spiritual things—I was *completely* ignorant of them. But Jesus Christ came into my life in 1970 and dramatically turned it around. I began preaching about a year and a half after my conversion, and I was pastoring at the ripe old age of nineteen. It seems crazy, doesn't it? But it happened.

We recently celebrated twenty-five years of ministry. As I look back on my life, I don't know what I would have done much differently. It was never our goal, per se, but we have become one of the largest churches in the country, with some fifteen thousand attending on an average Sunday. We see an average of three to four thousand people come to Christ every year in our church services alone. Thousands of others come to faith through our various outreach ministries, including the Harvest Crusades. One-fourth of the people in our congregation are actively involved in some type of ministry today. More than 60 percent of them came to faith at our services.

I know what you're thinking: This guy's bragging, and he's going to try to get me to buy into some program or seminar that will tell me how to do it for a small fee. And if I act now, he'll throw in some Ginsu knives! I guess I am bragging a little bit. But if I am, I am bragging on God, because I am about as ordinary a guy as you are going to meet. And that is why I have written this book. To give hope and some words of encouragement on how God can do extraordinary things through very ordinary people—people like me and maybe you. In this book I will share with you our theology, philosophy of ministry, and some practical advice as well.

I have been asked many times what verse best sums up my life and ministry. There are many things that I would love to quote that would position me as someone with great vision or faith. But if I were totally honest, it would be 1 Corinthians 1:26-29 (NIV): "Brothers, think of what you were when you were called. Not many of you were wise by human standards; not many were influential; not many were of noble birth. But God chose the foolish things of the world to shame the wise; God chose the weak things of the world to shame the strong. He chose the lowly things of this world and the despised things—and the things that are not—to nullify the things that are, so that no one may boast before him."

It is hard to explain all that the Lord has faithfully done in our ministry over the last twenty-five years. I'm reminded of a statement Warren Wiersbe made: "If you can explain what is going on then God didn't do it." I think there's truth to that. God has blessed our ministry. Yet we didn't use many of the techniques being touted today—surveys, studies, or attempts to have a more "friendly" approach to unbelievers. If you came to a service at Harvest Christian Fellowship, it would probably seem very contemporary to you. We have a relatively simple building, with no religious symbols to speak of. The music is clearly contemporary, and the dress style is casual. But underneath all of that are timeless biblical principles. This ministry could be compared to a

Windows 98 operating system. On the surface it is brightly colored, with simple icons to click. But underneath it is a DOS infrastructure. A healthy and thriving church must have a strong infrastructure. If you don't have a good foundation, trouble is coming, regardless of your growth, be it numerical or financial.

I would like to tell you our story. It may surprise or even shock you at times. I think you will laugh a bit. It has been and continues to be an adventure.

Humble Beginnings

After I became a Christian, I was afraid that God might "call" me to preach. I feared that it would happen at a really awkward time, such as when I was standing in line at the supermarket. I thought that maybe the Lord would force me to turn to the people behind me and say something really clever like, "I see that some of you are purchasing bread today. You know, Jesus said, 'I am the bread of life. He who comes to Me shall never hunger, and he who believes in Me shall never thirst'" (John 6:35, NKJV). Then I could say something like, "How many of you would like to come to Jesus right now?" The thought of the whole thing terrified me.

The day I first preached publicly did come. But it was not in the supermarket. In fact, it happened as the result of a misunderstanding. The church I attended was holding a mass baptism down at a beach in Newport Beach, California. I thought it was later that day, but it had already taken place, and I had missed it. When I rolled out of bed that

WE DIDN'T UTILIZE MANY OF THE NEW TECHNIQUES BEING TOUTED TODAY—NO SURVEYS, STUDIES, OR ATTEMPTS TO HAVE A MORE "FRIENDLY" APPROACH TO UNBELIEVERS.

morning, it was a day like any other day—no visions, no audible voices from heaven, no signs or wonders. But that day was about to alter the course of my life. I arrived at the beach, and instead of finding a few thousand people, as would be gathered for a baptism, I found only a handful. I was disappointed to have missed the baptism but glad to find some fellow believers to sing and fellowship with. As I joined their group I quickly noticed that no one was really leading. One person would sing a song, and others would join. Then another would sing a song, and we would sing again. I had read a passage of Scripture that morning that was sort of burning inside, and I sensed God nudging me to share it with this little group.

"Excuse me, but I read a Scripture this morning that I would like to share!" I blurted out nervously. Everyone seemed agreeable to the idea, so I stammered away, and when I was done, I was so relieved. I was saying to the Lord, quietly in my heart, *Lord, thank you for that wonderful opportunity! I can't wait to tell some of my Christian friends how you used me.*

I thought I was done that day, but the Lord was just getting started. While I was speaking, a couple of girls had joined our little group. When I finished, one of them said to me, "Excuse me, Pastor, but we missed the baptism, and we were wondering if you could still baptize us?"

"Pastor"?—what, is this girl nuts? I thought. "I'm sorry, I am not a pastor, and I don't even know how to baptize someone!" I protested.

"But we want to be baptized. Can't you help us?"

And then the Lord gave me a great sense of peace and impressed it upon my heart to go ahead and do it. "Uh, OK, I guess I could do that. Umm, let's go on down to Pirate's Cove."

Pirate's Cove is a charming little natural amphitheater, a spot etched in rock overlooking a small beach. Many times during the year, Calvary Chapel would have hundreds sit up on the rocks and watch as Pastor Chuck Smith and others baptized people. I had been baptized there myself, so it held fond memories for me. Except this time I was leading a little group that had now grown to about thirty down to Pirate's Cove, and I had no idea what I was going to do once I got there. As we went to the water's edge, I racked my brain, trying to remember something I had never really paid much attention to. The actual technique of baptizing a person! I remembered watching Pastor Chuck Smith holding a person's nose as he supported his back and gently lowered them backwards into the water. So I did the same and awkwardly baptized the first girl. She was still breathing afterwards, and I was greatly relieved. Then I baptized the second and was starting to feel like an old pro! As I came out of the water once again, I quietly rejoiced in this wonderful opportunity God had opened up for me.

While I was preparing to leave, I noticed that a crowd had gathered up on the rocks, taking all of this in. Then the thing I feared most came upon me. God clearly spoke to my heart and said one thing: "Preach!" Instead of being terrified, I had a great sense of calm and to the best of my ability proclaimed the gospel in my first little crusade. I even invited people to come down to where we were and receive Christ. A few did, and I had the privilege of baptizing them that day, too. Now I was ruined. I had the bug. Deep down, I knew that I was called to do this.

Early Days at Calvary

In those early growth days I couldn't get enough Bible study. I had no hostilities or hang-ups about the church because I knew nothing of it. In fact, I was like a sponge, drinking it all in and loving it. I wanted to serve the Lord somehow, and the only real skill I had to speak of was in graphic arts. In fact, my goal in life up to that point had been to become a professional cartoonist. Most of the Christian literature back in those days was pretty outdated. It was way out of step with the culture and, frankly, embarrassing to hand out.

So one day I decided to take one of Chuck Smith's sermons on John 4 and illustrate it in an easy-to-read comic-book format. I called it "Living Water." I wrote and drew it in about two hours and was so excited, I went over to his house and knocked on front door. When he came to the door, I held out my primitive little drawing and told him a bit about it. He really seemed to like the piece and suggested I redraw it in a tractlike format and then it could be printed up and distributed to the church. We printed about 10,000, and they were gone in a week. We printed 100,000, and they were soon gone. When all was said and done, upwards of 2 million of those little tracts had made their way out. Now I was really ruined. I knew that I was called to serve the Lord.

I began to support myself doing graphic arts on the side, but my real hope was to preach and teach others about Jesus Christ. I hung around Calvary Chapel, just hoping for opportunities to come my way. I set up my drawing board in one of the extra Sunday school rooms and would just wait for anything to do. When the pastors went out for lunch, I would firmly plant myself in the church office, hoping the secretary might shoot a counseling call or two my way. When a speaking opportunity arose in some faraway city no one wanted to go to, the other pastors would say, "Let Greg go. This would be a great opportunity for him!" I didn't mind a bit. I was eager to be used.

One day the ultimate leftover was dropped in my lap.

Leftovers from Heaven

An Episcopal church in a city called Riverside wanted to see if what God was doing in the Jesus movement down in Orange County could happen in their city as well. Some of the leaders of that church approached Chuck Smith and asked if he would send up some of the associate pastors to teach a Bible study aimed at young people. They rotated, each doing it for a few weeks and then handing it off to another. One particular week no one really wanted to go. They were talking about it among themselves as I quietly listened. One of the pastors said, "Hey, why not have Greg go up there?" They all agreed and said I could take the next Sunday night. I studied hard that week and desperately wanted to do well.

When I showed up at the church, I quickly realized no one had told them I was coming. They were expecting a pastor they already knew. The elder in charge reluctantly agreed to have me preach and said that he would be watching and listening very closely that night. Not exactly a vote of confidence! But I made my way through it and was told I could come back again the next week. So each week I spoke, and attendance actually began to grow. People started to receive Christ, and I was beside myself with joy! In fact, it grew into a group of about three hundred, and some of the people were starting to call me Pastor Greg. Here was the "pastor" thing again. It was almost laughable. I was twenty years old! I had been a Christian for only three years. I hardly felt qualified to be a pastor. Besides, I really felt called to evangelism, not pastoring. But this crazy Bible study just kept growing.

This little Bible study that I had the privilege of leading had now, for all practical purposes, become a church. We had outgrown the facilities at the Episcopal church where we began, so we looked for our own building. I was told of a Baptist church in the middle of town that had had a split and was available for lease or rent. We had no money in the bank and were really a bunch of kids just trying to do what we thought God wanted us to do. I called Chuck Smith and asked him if he would come and check this thing out with me. As we walked around the building, taking it all in, Chuck spoke with the Realtor who had listed it. I saw Chuck take out his checkbook, write out a check, and hand it to the Realtor. They shook hands, and Chuck came over to me and said, "Well, congratulations, Greg. You just got yourself a church!" He had to get back to Costa Mesa, so he climbed into his car and drove out of the parking lot, and I just stood there stunned.

What was I going to do? Who was going to help me? Was I really called to do this? As it turned out, Pastor Chuck had provided the down payment, but the rest was up to us. The next Sunday we made the announcement at the Episcopal church that we were moving to this new building. I was terrified that no one would follow us. But the next week they showed up in force. We were now five hundred strong!

I felt called primarily as an evangelist. Prior to taking on this Bible study, in addition to doing graphics I had become something of an itinerant preacher. I traveled with a number of the early contemporary Christian music groups, and I sort of emceed the evening and then got up and preached the gospel and gave an invitation for people to come to Christ. As itinerant, or traveling, preachers often do, I had developed five or six messages that I gave over and over, and they were well honed.

Yet now, here I was, called upon to teach every single week in the same place in this new and growing church that I had somehow become the pastor of. We had not only our Sunday night services but Wednesday services as well. I had to learn how to really study. I decided to teach through the books of the Bible as I had seen modeled at Calvary Chapel. I decided to start with Ephesians. The commentary *In the Heavenlies,* by Harry Ironside, was recommended to me, and I used that as my guide. For all practical purposes I stole Ironside's outlines, illustrations, and antidotes lock, stock, and barrel, but I was beginning to develop my own style. The numbers were not huge for our midweek studies, but I gave my all, sometimes learning things for the first time as I prepared during the day and delivered it to the people who came out that night.

Sunday nights were another issue altogether. I gave all my traveling messages and some new ones I developed and invited people to come to Christ as I had done on the road. But the response was dismal. I soon realized that these people needed to be fed the Word of God, and healthy sheep would reproduce themselves. So on Sunday nights, instead of topical evangelistic messages, I taught through books like the Gospel of John, Revelation, Genesis, Daniel, etc. Then I still gave an invitation for people to come to Christ. Now they were responding. And we began to grow even more.

You have probably noticed that I did not mention Sunday morning yet. This is because, as strange as it may sound, we did not yet have a Sunday-morning service. We were still largely a group of young people meeting together, and we decided we ought to do some kind of outreach for the older folks. What a reverse of what we normally hear! Instead of older people trying to reach the young, here were young people trying to reach the old. I hardly felt qualified, being only twenty-one at the time. So I asked a friend of mine who was in his fifties to teach on Sunday mornings; I could do the Sunday evenings and Wednesdays.

*C*HUCK CAME OVER TO ME AND SAID, "WELL, CONGRATULATIONS, GREG. YOU JUST GOT YOURSELF A CHURCH!"

The Sunday-morning services averaged about sixty people in attendance. This was odd, considering that we were running about a thousand in our evening service at that point. This man, Keith, had a wonderful heart and gave it his all, but to be honest, I think God wanted me to be preaching that service, too. I sort of used Keith as a security blanket because I was so apprehensive about speaking to a more adult audience. One week Keith had a heart attack. He was not able to do the Sunday-morning services, so I was on. (Keith recovered and was called to mission work in China—God has plans for everybody!) I continued teaching Sunday mornings, and the Lord blessed our efforts. Today our Sunday morning services are our best attended.

Evangelistic Doors Open: The Harvest Crusades

We have always given people an opportunity to come to Christ in our services. In fact, most of our associate pastors either came to faith at our church or began attending as very young believers. We have seen thousands and thousands walk the aisles over the years to make a commitment or recommitment to follow Jesus Christ. You might say our philosophy of ministry, in a nutshell, would be to know Christ and make him known.

Our Sunday evening service was always a bit more evangelistic than the others, and it was still my desire to see large-scale outreaches in our community. We booked a relatively large auditorium in a neighboring city and held our first crusade-type meetings, which we called Harvest celebrations back then. The Lord blessed, and we saw many respond. But as hard as I tried, I could not get those events to the next level, where other churches would come on board and help. I just stopped worrying about it and got on with doing the job of a pastor that God had set before me.

I read a story about young Charles Spurgeon, who had some visions of grandeur for himself and his ministry that was opening up in London. The Lord reminded him of a passage in Jeremiah: "Do you seek great things for yourself? Do not seek them" (Jer. 45:5, NKJV). It's hard not to be accused of egotism when you suggest that a huge meeting be held and you are to be the one doing the preaching. I just stopped worrying about trying to make it happen and concluded that maybe this was not God's will for my life. I was reminded of Paul's words when he said, "I have learned in whatever state I am, to be content" (Phil. 4:11, NKJV). There is a real temptation for those of us who are called to serve the Lord to see the grass as greener elsewhere—to think that bigger is always better. That we should be moving up some sort of ladder of spiritual success. But I have found, in retrospect, that we should be thankful for any opportunity God has opened up for us, no matter how large or small it may be. As Warren

Wiersbe has said, "You can never be too small for God to use, only too big."

What God requires of us is faithfulness. And if we are "faithful in the little things," He will give us more to do in His perfect timing. Scripture reminds us to not despise "the day of small things" (Zech. 4:10, NKJV). You are learning important lessons—lessons you will treasure for years to come—through what God is doing in your life right now. A minister of a smaller church once met the great C. H. Spurgeon, who was at the zenith of his ministry, and complained about the small size of his congregation. The minister voiced his envy of the thousands who came to hear Spurgeon each week. Spurgeon asked him, "How many people attend your church?" The minister replied, "About one hundred." Spurgeon replied, "I think that is enough to give an account of on the Day of Judgment." Ouch! What has God set before you right now? A home Bible study? A Sunday-school class? A small congregation? An individual you are discipling? That's enough to give an account of on the Day of Judgment!

As Warren Wiersbe has said, "You can never be too small for God to use, only too big."

It was when I honestly found this contentment in what God had put on my plate that some very unexpected opportunities opened up for us to touch not only our community but also our state and our nation. They were to be called Harvest Crusades.

Like so many other things in my life, the opportunity to do crusades came when I least expected it. Chuck Smith asked if I would speak at a Monday night Bible study at Calvary Chapel, a study he had led for many years. I had attended it myself. It was a great honor to be asked to do this, and though our church was going strong and there were many things pulling on me, I sensed the Lord's leading to go for it. I applied the same format we have used for years at Harvest on Sunday nights: a time of contemporary praise and worship; often a guest musical artist (not usually announced ahead of time); and then a forty-five- to sixty-minute Bible study with evangelism woven through it.

Before we knew it, we were averaging twenty-five hundred people each Monday night, with anywhere from forty to eighty people coming to Christ each week. We were thrilled with the response. This would be great on a Sunday or Wednesday night midweek study, but Monday night? After this had gone on for about a year, I was at a meeting with some other pastors down in Costa Mesa, and Chuck Smith took me aside for a moment and dropped something on me that would change the course of my life and ministry. In his matter-of-fact way he said, "Greg, I've been noticing the Lord's blessing on the Monday-night studies this last year and thought we should take it to a larger venue, say, the Pacific Amphitheater, and do a Billy Graham–style crusade."

I was dumbfounded. "Isn't the Pacific Amphitheater a pretty big place, Chuck?" I asked.

"Yes, Greg, it is," Chuck said, with a twinkle in his eye. Then he added, "But we serve a big God!"

We had no idea how many people to expect for that first crusade. I wanted to take what God had been blessing in our Sunday-/Monday-night studies and combine it with some tried-and-true principles of large-scale evangelism. I had long studied the ministries of evangelists like D. L. Moody and Billy Graham. I wanted this crusade to build on the principles of what God had blessed over the years, combined with contemporary style and music. So we went about designing a new approach to the crusade format. My associate, John Collins, helped to brilliantly execute this first event and continues as our crusade director to this very day. The Lord has been faithful these last ten years, and we have seen over 2 million people in combined attendance, and over 150,000 people have walked the aisles to make commitments and recommitments to follow Jesus Christ.

After the crusade ministry began taking off, I was often asked when I was going to leave the pastorate and go into full-time evangelism. It seemed like the next logical step to everyone, even, at times, to myself. Yet, strangely, the very thing I had dreamed of for so many years held no appeal to me whatsoever. I loved (and still love) going out and sharing the gospel in venues large and small. At the same time, given a choice, I prefer to speak to our own congregation. I enjoy the interaction, the rapport, the contact of speaking to a group of people you can actually make eye contact with. In a stadium, all you see are little dots, and your voice bounces back to you as you speak. I'm not complaining. It is thrilling to see hundreds of people come forward to put their faith in Christ. But there is a price to pay for it, and that's another story I would like to tell at another time.

WHAT WE NOW CONSIDER TO BE RADICAL BEHAVIOR WAS TO EARLY BELIEVERS NOTHING MORE THAN A SINCERE ATTEMPT TO LIVE OBEDIENTLY.

The First Disciples: Radical or Right?
Let me ask you a question. Do you really want to change the world? You might be thinking, *Of course I do, Greg, but I'm a pretty ordinary person. Most days I can hardly manage to change my printer cartridge, much less the world.*

I understand that response. But consider this: Two millennia ago a group of believers, led by twelve men armed with little more than the message of the gospel, turned the world completely upside down. This was a relatively small group of believers who began meeting in an obscure upstairs room. They lacked almost every advantage we enjoy today. They didn't have mass media, computer and satellite technology, or stadium rallies. They didn't have the ability to publish their materials or the financial resources to build beautiful cathedrals.

And yet the church these Christians founded together in that small room upstairs not only survived but flourished. While being attacked spiritually and physically, this small group of men and women spread the message of salvation abroad and performed countless miracles in Christ's name. From every possible perspective—spiritual, historical, political—they left the world a different place from the way they had found it.

You might say, "These guys weren't like you and me. They were a bunch of radicals, right?"

Not at all. In fact, here's a truly radical thought: The early church leaders were simply living their Christian lives according to what Jesus taught. *What we consider to be radical behavior was nothing more than a sincere attempt to live obediently.* What many of us consider normal Christian living today—compared to what the first church experienced—is not normal at all. It's woefully inadequate and, as a result, pitifully ineffective.

When unbelievers said of the early Christians that they "turned the world upside down" (Acts 17:6, NKJV), it was clearly not meant as a compliment. In fact, it was an accusation and a criticism. Everywhere the disciples preached the gospel of Christ, they upset the norm. They changed the way people saw religion, God, politics, church, and personal relationships.

Jesus said in John 18:36: "My kingdom is not of this world. If it were, my servants would fight to prevent my arrest by the Jews. But now my kingdom is from another place" (NIV). He was saying, in essence, "My people aren't going to act the way you expect because I operate from completely different principles and goals."

Then, as now, it was really the sinful people whose ideas were all turned around, backwards, and upside down. So when the early Christians were said to be turning the world upside down, they were actually putting *right* what had been wrong since the fall of humanity in the Garden of Eden.

This is why the greatest compliment the church today could receive would be to have people complain that we Christians are turning the world on its ear. And if we aren't being accused of this, it's most likely because we're operating according to the principles of this world instead of according to God's upside-down kingdom principles.

Of course, most Christians and churches readily agree, on an intellectual level, with the principles Jesus taught. But how we respond in everyday life is usually another matter. How many of us truly love Him more than anything or anyone else, or really take up our cross daily and follow Him?

Yet anything short of this kind of "radical" discipleship—which is really what ordinary Christian living should be—is settling for less than what God desires.

CAPPUCCINO OR CHURCH?

Question: If Christians are the body of Christ, then why does church need to be in a building called "church"? Why can't I just have fellowship with a friend over lattes?

Answer: Many people question the validity of the church as an institution. But the church is the only organization that Jesus himself established.

Church is an *of course* to Jesus. It was also an *of course* to the early apostles. They encouraged one another, wrote to one another, exhorted one another. Paul agonized, in fact, about his desire to go and be with Christ versus his desire to be on earth with the church, his first family.

Of the church, Jesus said, "The gates of hell shall not prevail against it" (Matt. 16:18, KJV).

Unfortunately many of us hardly care about the church at large. We feel entitled to a good church, but most of us aren't doing anything more than spectating. We want the pastor's sermons to be good, but we also want them short because we have other things we want to do on Sunday besides warm the pews.

Instead of asking, "Why do I have to go to church?" we should be asking, "What can I do to minister to and build up Christ's own precious body, of which I am a part?"

I heard the story of a husband and wife who got up one Sunday morning as usual to get ready for church. It was just about time to walk out the door, and the wife noticed that her husband wasn't even dressed yet. She asked, "Why aren't you getting ready for church?"

"'Cause I don't want to go!"

"Do you have any reasons?"

"Yes, I have three good reasons. First, the congregation is cold. Second, no one likes me. And third, I just don't want to go."

The wife replied, wisely, "Well, honey, I have three reasons you *should* go. First, the congregation is warm. Second, there are a few people there who like you. And third, you're the pastor! So get dressed!"

What Kind of Person Can This Book Help?

Maybe you're a young Christian who's excited about living out your faith with your new family of faith—but you don't know where to start. What should you expect? How can you plug in?

Maybe you're a longtime Christian who feels ineffective or hampered at every turn. Too often your church body behaves just like the world you're trying to influence. Some days you feel as if you all got a new paint job but underneath you're still the same old Plymouth. How can you be like one of those first-century "upside-down" believers?

Or maybe you're among the many Christians in the so-called boomer and buster generations who have grown a bit cynical. You're not so much disappointed with God as you are disappointed with church. I mean, why put up with confusing liturgies and trite sermons? Why be associated—even remotely—with some of those TV preachers who wave Bibles but look and act like idiots? Along with plenty of friends, you're thinking, *Why should I even attend?*

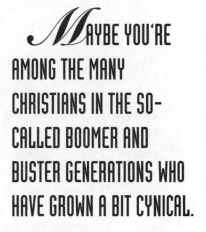

*M*AYBE YOU'RE AMONG THE MANY CHRISTIANS IN THE SO-CALLED BOOMER AND BUSTER GENERATIONS WHO HAVE GROWN A BIT CYNICAL.

Perhaps you are a pastor who is trying to understand why nothing seems to be happening in your church. People aren't turning their lives over to Jesus Christ and being transformed; attendance is down; morale is low. Is this all your call to ministry is supposed to amount to? Should you bring in a marketing firm? Should you stop saying *Jesus* so much?

If you find yourself in any of these profiles, this book is for you. My prayer is that it can be part of God's plan to nudge you, along with other believers in your life, toward the kind of church experience that Jesus had in mind.

In some ways you might say that this book is a "church growth" book. However, my goal is not to show you how to be part of a church that is growing numerically or is catering to a certain segment of society. My goal is to show you how to be part of an "upside-down" church that is growing in power and impact because it has healthy foundations and operates according to God's kingdom principles.

The principles I want to share with you may not be what

you'd expect. I won't be proposing that you learn to do church exactly the way we do it at Harvest Christian Fellowship, although I often use our church as an example. I won't be telling you how to double the size of your congregation necessarily, although I believe a healthy church will naturally grow.

What I will be saying is that we don't need more programs or slick techniques. These principles aren't "Greg's Gimmicks for Success" or the latest buzz at some cutting-edge seminary. Instead, my intention is that everything you read will be timely and contemporary but at the same time completely biblical.

The Foolish Power of God

When I came to faith, God didn't exactly catch a big fish for Himself. I wasn't a celebrity. I wasn't a former this or a former that. I was a mixed-up seventeen-year-old. But God took this ordinary kid and turned his life around.

Let me tell you a little story that took place when I was in high school. No sooner had I become a Christian than I decided I didn't want to hang out with what we used to call the "Jesus freaks." In my newly converted state, they seemed just a little too intense for me, talking nonstop about God and quoting Scripture all the time. I thought, *I don't know if I want to go that far. I think I'm going to go solo. Me and God. We will work it out.*

One day, shortly after this, I was walking across the campus, and some guy approached me and said, "Brother Greg, I have something for you. I got you a Bible, bro!"

It was one of the Christian guys I didn't really want to hang out with. He held up this large, cowhide-covered Bible with two Popsicle sticks glued in the shape of a cross on the front. "I want you to have this, brother," He said, obviously very pleased with himself.

I said, "Oh, gee, thanks. What am I supposed to do with this?"

"Start reading it, brother. It's the Word of God!"

My eyes darted around, hoping no one would see me talking

with this guy. It's not that I did not have respect for the Bible; I just didn't want to carry one around on my high school campus. And certainly not one with Popsicle sticks glued together in the shape of a cross!

The fact is, I was embarrassed. As soon as this guy walked away, I shoved the Bible into my coat pocket so hard I ripped the seams. I was on my way over to a friend's house, and I certainly didn't want to be caught with this thing.

When I got to the door of my friend's house, I noticed a planter out front with some bushes in it. I looked to the left. I looked to the right. I pulled the Bible out and hid it in the bushes.

When my friend opened the door, I walked in, trying to look cool. Several of my friends were there. "Hey, guys," I said. "How's it going?"

"Hey, Greg, where have you been lately?"

"Nowhere." My heart was beating fast. I didn't want to tell them that I'd decided to be a Christian.

Then one of the guys said, "Do you want to go get stoned?"

"No. No. Not at all."

"What's wrong with you?"

"Nothing is wrong. I'm totally fine." They were all looking at me as if I'd lost my mind when suddenly the front door flew open and there stood this guy's mother. She asked, "Who does this belong to?" and held up the big cowhide Bible with the Popsicle-stick cross on the front. Every eye in the room looked at the Bible, and then every eye in the room looked at me.

"It's mine," I said sheepishly.

My so-called friends had a great laugh at my expense. One of them said, "Oh, praise the Lord, brother Greg! Are you going to be a nice Christian boy now and read the Bible, pray, and go to church?"

"No, I'm going to hit you in the mouth right now if you don't shut up!" (I hadn't yet read the part in the Bible about loving people.)

This was especially hard for me to take because I was always the mocker in school. I was the guy with the fast quip and smart-alecky response to the teacher. I had raised mockery to an art form. And now I, the mocker extraordinaire, was the one being mocked.

But I realized that if I was going to be a real follower of Jesus Christ, I had to make a break with these old buddies.

I would realize later that this Bible I was so ashamed of was the very Word of God that would change my life and the lives of others I would have the privilege of sharing its message with.

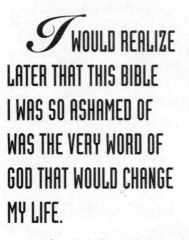

I WOULD REALIZE LATER THAT THIS BIBLE I WAS SO ASHAMED OF WAS THE VERY WORD OF GOD THAT WOULD CHANGE MY LIFE.

And you know what? Nothing's been the same since. Now that Bible I was ashamed to hold up is the book I speak from. It is my only authority, and it contains the only message I proclaim. As Paul said, "I am not ashamed of the gospel of Christ, for it is the power of God to salvation for everyone who believes" (Rom. 1:16, NKJV).

I firmly believe that God can turn any life upside down, just as He did mine. And through the "foolishness" of those who are willing to follow him, God can remake your church experience. He can turn the course of a generation and a world—one silly Popsicle-stick cross at a time.

"You Have a Little Strength"
We've been talking about the first church, which is described in the book of Acts. But when we look at a description of the church of the last days, which I believe we are a part of, the message of Jesus to the church in Philadelphia is relevant to us.

*To the angel of the church in Philadelphia write,
"These things says He who is holy, He who is true,
'He who has the key of David, He who opens and no
one shuts, and shuts and no one opens': I know your
works. See, I have set before you an open door, and
no one can shut it; for you have a little strength, have
kept My word, and have not denied My name." Rev.
3:7-8, NKJV*

There are a number of ways we can interpret what Jesus means by "I have set before you an open door." But one way is that He is speaking of a door of unprecedented opportunity. Paul used this same picture in 2 Corinthians 2:12, where He says, "I came to Troas to preach Christ's gospel, and a door was opened to me by the Lord" (NKJV).

In essence, Jesus is saying to His followers, "Hey, look. I have opened a door for you. What will you do with it?"

Today we have a unique opportunity to get the gospel out. Countries that were previously closed are now open. And we have technology to project the gospel message to more people than ever before.

But just as important are the doors that are open in your own life. Are you seeing the openings among family members or people you work with? Are you sensing God's call to walk forward into a bold new way of living out your faith?

ARE YOU SENSING GOD'S CALL TO WALK FORWARD INTO A BOLD NEW WAY OF LIVING OUT YOUR FAITH?

The next thing Jesus says to the church is, "You have a little strength." This is very much like the picture of a sick person coming back to life. You know what it is like to lie around when you have a fever. If you jump to your feet too quickly, your head throbs, and you wobble a little bit. But you know you're getting better because you feel your strength coming back.

Jesus uses this image to describe the church of the last days. We're not a superchurch. We're not a perfect church. But we are a church that is coming back to life. And you are a key part of that church.

Will you accept God's challenge to penetrate this culture and not be ashamed of this life-changing message God has given us? It is the only hope for America.

PASTOR TO PASTOR

From the Inside Out

A lot of good books about how to do church take an approach that works from the outside in.

Let's face it. A lot of pastors don't have money to finance a demographic survey. Maybe you've tried every possible technique to get your church to feel that it's going somewhere, but your congregation is still letting out one long yawn.

In this book I'm more interested in the heart of the church, the passion of its people, the inner fire that changes things *in spite of size, programs, or numbers.* Too many of us are caught up in the outside stuff—focusing on numbers, building programs, and the latest ways to attract new members. And in the process, we've lost sight of our first love. We've lost our light, our burning fire, to see people turn to Christ.

What I'm proposing is something simple. It's too basic to be impressive. It should be easy—even obvious—but it's not. And so I hope to help you dig beneath the layers of "church" to get to the heart of what makes any church a force to be reckoned with—regardless of size.

I firmly believe that a vital small-town church that is ignited for God is far more capable of setting the world on fire than a huge church that has turned into a social club.

For the Believer in Jesus Who Wants an Upside-Down Life
Listen. The observers are many. The critics are many. The fair-weather followers are many. The compromisers are many. But the laborers are few. Will you become a laborer? No one can honestly pray for this work to be done who is not willing to help do it.

Perhaps you feel that your spiritual resume is weak. Maybe, like Peter, you smell of fish. Or maybe your church's resumé falls short of the mark, and you wonder if it can rise to God's challenge. Maybe you've tried so many times before that you're reluctant to pin your hopes again on what God can do. But God has purposefully put in your heart those hopes for how His people can have an impact on the world.

WE'RE NOT A PERFECT CHURCH. BUT WE ARE A CHURCH THAT IS COMING BACK TO LIFE.

Will you ask the Holy Spirit to stir your heart to answer the desire of Jesus? Will you pray, "Lord, use me"?

The story is told of an old preacher who was aboard that fateful trip on the *Titanic*. After he was thrown into the freezing Atlantic, he swam from lifeboat to lifeboat, raft to raft, piece of ship to piece of ship, crying out to people, "Trust Christ. Take Him as Savior. Receive Him into your heart. Call upon the name of the Lord, and you will be saved."

Today people are drowning all around those of us who are safe in Christ. We need to follow the example of this old preacher and get out the message: Trust Christ!

Remember, God makes us able to do whatever He's called us to do. And we have *a little strength*—exactly enough to turn our country, our town, our church, our neighborhood, our family, and ourself upside down for Christ.

TWO

A FEW GOOD CHRISTIANS
How Twelve Men Turned
the World on Its Ear

LET'S TAKE a closer look now at those first-century believers and see if we can get a handle on what they believed and did.

They lived upside-down lives, walking in obedience to God and applying the truths of His kingdom. Here's another way to look at it: God has told us, "My thoughts are not your thoughts, nor are your ways My ways" (Isa. 55:8, NKJV). In fact, most of the time God's purposes are exactly the opposite of our human impulses.

This means that in order to truly follow Him we must think and behave in ways that feel unnatural, or upside down, to us. This is what the early church did. How did they do it? In Acts 2:42-47, we find a snapshot of how the early church was working.

> *They continued steadfastly in the apostles' doctrine and fellowship, in the breaking of bread, and in prayers. Then fear came upon every soul, and many wonders and signs were done through the apostles. Now all who believed were together, and had all things in common, and sold their possessions and goods, and divided them among all, as anyone had need. So continuing daily with one accord in the temple, and breaking bread from house to house, they ate their food with gladness and simplicity of heart, praising God*

*and having favor with all the people. And the Lord added
to the church daily those who were being saved.* NKJV

When we read this passage or think of the disciples, as well as
the early apostles like Paul, we tend to see them as superhuman.
We imagine saintly figures in stained glass, people who were
somehow different from the rank and file of humanity.

But any honest examination of
the Scriptures reveals just the opposite. They were ordinary people
who were subject to the same
weaknesses and shortcomings we
all experience. Jesus appeared to
go out of His way to find a group
of followers who had little claim to
greatness apart from their willingness to believe and obey Him.

*IF YOU WERE GOING
TO SELECT A DOZEN GUYS
TO CHANGE THE WORLD,
WOULD YOU HAVE PICKED
THE GROUP JESUS PICKED?*

If you were going to select a
dozen guys to change the world, would you have picked the
group Jesus picked? Imagine if Jesus submitted the resumes of
His team to a modern management group. The results might
read something like this:

> *Thank you for submitting the resumes of the twelve men
> you're considering for management positions in your
> new organization. All of them have taken our battery
> of tests, the results of which we've run through sophisti-
> cated computer analyses. We've also arranged personal
> interviews for each candidate with our psychologist and
> vocational-aptitude consultant.*
>
> *It is our staff's unanimous opinion that most of the
> nominees are lacking in qualifications for the type of
> enterprise you are undertaking. We recommend that
> you continue your search for persons of experience and
> managerial ability and proven capability.*

We find that Simon Peter is emotionally unstable and given to fits of temper. He seems far too impulsive to be put in a position of oversight. Andrew has absolutely no qualities of leadership. The brothers James and John place personal interest above company loyalty. And they seem to be impatient with others. Due to this impatience and ambition, they could one day become disgruntled employees.

Thomas demonstrates a questioning attitude that could tend to undermine morale. We feel it is our duty to tell you that Matthew has been blacklisted by the Greater Jerusalem Better Business Bureau.

In closing, one of the candidates shows great potential. He is a man of ability, resourcefulness, and ambition. We recommend Judas Iscariot as your comptroller and right-hand man. All the other profiles are self-explanatory.

Sincerely yours,
Jordan Management Consultants, Jerusalem

These were the men God put His hand upon and used to turn the world upside down! And just imagine how Saul of Tarsus, who later became Paul the apostle, would have fared as a candidate for Jesus' team.

Once again we see how God's ways are upside down to us.

As we look at the people God used in Scripture and in contemporary history, we see that God has always gone out of His way to find individuals who didn't look as though they would amount to much. This is great news because it gives you and me assurance that God can use us just as surely and as powerfully as He used those men and women.

> GOD HAS ALWAYS GONE OUT OF HIS WAY TO FIND INDIVIDUALS WHO DIDN'T LOOK AS THOUGH THEY WOULD AMOUNT TO MUCH.

In fact, the Bible tells us, "The eyes of the Lord run to and fro throughout the whole earth, to show Himself strong on behalf of those whose heart is loyal to Him" (2 Chron. 16:9, NKJV). It doesn't say He is looking for a strong man or a strong woman but rather someone whom *He* could be strong *on behalf of.*

So how do we become the kind of person—or the kind of church—God is searching for?

When we look to the disciples, we can see three things that made them people God could use to build His upside-down church.

- They walked according to the Spirit, not the flesh (human inclinations).
- They kept in mind the purposes of God, not the priorities of people.
- They acted according to God's methods, not their own.

According to the Spirit

I believe one key reason the church is not affecting the world today as it ought is that it is not relying on the Holy Spirit. Far too often we are relying on programs or on surveys and entertainment. We are relying on other means instead of depending on the Holy Spirit to do His work. As a result, we fail. We can't turn this world upside down on our own power.

People who have put their faith in Christ have had the Holy Spirit come to live within them. He dwells inside them. But Jesus promises a dimension of power even beyond this. In Acts 1:8, He said, "But you shall receive power when the Holy Spirit has come upon you; and you shall be witnesses to Me in Jerusalem, and in all Judea and Samaria, and to the end of the earth." (NKJV)

Jesus was saying here that we need this power to gain supernatural courage and boldness to be witnesses. When we are filled with the Spirit, He gives us a supernatural power to know and do His will, to share the gospel, to resist temptation, and to live a life that is pleasing to God.

The word *filled,* specifically in Ephesians 5, where it says, "Be filled with the Spirit," has many shades of meaning. One translation of the word is the idea of the wind's filling the sail of a ship as it carries the ship out to sea. So to be filled with the Spirit is to allow God to fill your sails and guide your course through life, with His commands being sources not of drudgery but of delight.

But in the original language the idea of being filled with the Spirit also implies something being permeated. The picture here is that God wants His Holy Spirit to permeate the lives of His children in what they say, think, and do. It is not some emotional experience or a brief time during which I am filled with the Spirit.

*W*E ARE RELYING ON PROGRAMS OR ON SURVEYS AND ENTERTAINMENT INSTEAD OF DEPENDING UPON THE HOLY SPIRIT TO DO HIS WORK.

To be filled with the Spirit means that God's Spirit is infiltrating every aspect of your life. He is permeating your prayer life and your worship life. He is permeating your business, too, and the way you treat others. He is permeating all that you say and do. To be filled with the Spirit means that I am carried along by, and under the control of, Jesus Christ. It means I fill myself with the Word of God so that His thoughts become my thoughts, His standards my standards, His will my will. When we are filled with the Spirit, we are walking thought by thought, decision by decision, act by act, under the Spirit's control.

This implies an ongoing process. We are being filled again and again.

Let's suppose someone you know just bought a new car, and after a week it stopped running. The person says, "This piece of junk! I can't believe it—it just stopped running."

"Really?" you say. "When was the last time you put gas in it?"

"When I bought it."

"Have you gone to the gas station since then?"

"No."

The problem is not the car. The car simply needs its gas tank refilled. And the tank will need to be refilled as long as the owner wishes to drive around in it.

A lot of churches and individuals are wondering what is wrong with their lives. They put the key in the ignition, but it won't start. Maybe it's just time for a refill. You need to be filled with the Spirit. Don't misunderstand; God doesn't supply His power merely so that we can have an emotional experience. He doesn't give us His power just so we can feel good about ourselves or have a wonderful time at church. The Holy Spirit's power is the practical means for us to have an impact on the world. Every person should pray that God will fill him or her with His Spirit today.

THE SPIRIT DOESN'T GIVE US POWER JUST SO THAT WE CAN FEEL GOOD ABOUT OURSELVES OR HAVE A WONDERFUL TIME AT CHURCH.

And every pastor should pray, "Lord, there is no way we can make a difference in our culture through our own strength. We can't do it through programs or gimmicks. We can't do it through any of our own devices. We need a power beyond ourselves."

CHRISTIANS ANONYMOUS

Question: Greg, I'm a little turned off to the whole church scene—at least as we see it here in the States. Look at TV Christianity. Look at mainline denominations "blessing" same-sex marriages. Why shouldn't Christians distance themselves from the church?

Answer: True Christians should distance themselves from

any "church" that violates biblical standards. At the same time, we don't want to throw out the baby with the bathwater.

You want to find a church that has a balanced approach, which must include clear and strong biblical teaching, heartfelt and God-honoring worship, warm and loving fellowship, and vital, engaging evangelism.

The only "organization" Jesus ever started was the church. The day we received Him as Lord and Savior we became members of the body of Christ, or the church as a whole. We need the interaction, accountability, and outlet for our gifts and talents that only the local church can provide.

According to God's Purposes

The second principle we see at work in the disciples is that they walked according to God's purposes. But it didn't start out that way—at least not for all of them.

Remember Peter's mistake? When Jesus explained that He must go on to Jerusalem to suffer and die, Peter took Jesus aside and began to rebuke him. "Never, Lord!" he said. "This shall never happen to you!"

In many ways this was a natural response. When someone we love predicts that something terrible must happen, we want to say, "Oh no! Things are going to be fine." This was a genuine, well-intentioned response. But, unknown to Peter, there was another spirit behind it.

But Jesus turned and said to Peter, "Get behind me, Satan! You are a stumbling block to me; you do not have in mind the things of God, but the things of men" (Matt. 16:23, NIV).

This is one of the harshest rebukes recorded in Scripture, and it demonstrates an important point. If we miss this, we can be a stumbling block instead of a stepping-stone to furthering Christ's kingdom. *If we want to become part of an upside-down church, we have to keep in mind not our own priorities but God's.*

We can know Jesus well. We can even be walking with Him, loving Him, wanting to do what is right. But if we're just going along on our impulses, we're most likely going to do and say the opposite of what God has in mind.

*T*HROUGHOUT THE BIBLE, GOD REMINDS US TO CHANGE OUR THINKING, TO SEE WITH SPIRITUAL EYES, TO REMEMBER THAT HIS THOUGHTS ARE NOT OURS.

God's ways—His goals and purposes—are so radically different from ours. That is why we have to be ready to live and to think in ways that may feel upside down to us.

Throughout the Bible, God reminds us to change our thinking (among other things), to see with spiritual eyes, to remember that His thoughts are not ours. The Bible is, among other things, a collection of stories about people who discovered this. Consider Saul of Tarsus, Mary, Gideon, and Abraham. At some point they were surprised by what God had in mind. Imagine what some of their incredulous questions might have been:

- Gideon: "You want me to lead an army of three hundred against an army numbering well into the thousands?"
- Mary: "You want the Messiah to be born in a stable?"
- Abraham: "You want me to sacrifice my son Isaac?"
- Saul: "You want your worst enemy to preach to the Gentiles?"

What's on *your* mind? Insert your name below in place of the word *God* in the following list. If you're a pastor, repeat the process with the name of your church. Are the statements still true?

- God is more interested in God's eternal goals than in our temporary plans.
- God is more interested in what's in a person's heart than in what's in our religious practice.
- God is more interested in making us more like Jesus than in our temporary happiness or comfort.
- God always prioritizes the spiritual ahead of the physical.
- God is often more interested in revealing God through people's weaknesses than through their strengths.

According to God's Methods

We've seen that the disciples operated according to the Holy Spirit and according to God's purposes. But the third important thing we notice about the early Christians is their methods. They not only had in mind the things of God (Peter had learned his lesson!), but they went about accomplishing God's work in God's ways.

The first Christians didn't out-argue pagans—they outlived them. It is worth noting that Christianity made no attempts to conquer paganism and dead Judaism by reacting blow by blow. Instead, the Christians of the first century outthought, outprayed and outlived the unbelievers. Their weapons were positive, not negative.

As far as we know, they did not hold protests or conduct boycotts.

THE FIRST CHRISTIANS OUTTHOUGHT, OUTPRAYED, AND OUTLIVED THE UNBELIEVERS. THEIR WEAPONS WERE POSITIVE, NOT NEGATIVE.

They did not put on campaigns to try to unseat the emperor. Instead, they prayed and preached and proclaimed the message of Christ, put to death on the cross, risen from the dead, and ready to change lives. And they backed up their message with actions: giving, loving.

Today the church as a whole (I speak of the evangelical church in this context) has never been better organized politically across the country. We get the word out quickly through our grapevine when legislation comes up that is not good for the nation morally and spiritually. We speak up and make a difference. That is good.

But has our passion for what is temporarily good displaced our passion for going about God's business God's way? When did our *work* for Jesus begin to overtake our *worship* of Him? Are we more inclined to protest than we are to pray? Are we more interested in who is in the White House than in who is in God's house? Are we more interested in boycotts than we are in the salvation of family and friends?

Social and political action have their place; they are not wrong in themselves. But it's tempting to battle with only those weapons. Our primary weapons are spiritual, and our job is to be ambassadors to the world—ambassadors who understand our Leader's policies and employ only His upside-down tactics (taken from Matthew 5):

- Give to those who take.
- Love those who persecute us.
- Bless those who curse us.
- Humble ourselves.
- Lay down our life.

We are in a war. But it takes only a glance through this list to see how radically different God's weapons are from the weapons typically used in moral, political, and social battles.

The early Christians recognized this. They knew that the nature of their struggle was essentially spiritual, for "we do not wrestle against flesh and blood, but against principalities, against powers, against the rulers of the darkness of this age, against spiritual hosts of wickedness in the heavenly places" (Eph. 6:12, NKJV). And because of the spiritual nature of this struggle, they understood the spiritual nature of their weapons, as seen in 2 Corinthians 10:4: "The weapons we fight with are not the weapons of the world. On the contrary, they have divine power to demolish strongholds" (NIV).

As a result, the early Christians prevailed. Where is Rome today? There is still a place called Rome, but it is no longer a world power. Now it happens to be a very polluted tourist attraction. We go to Rome today to see the ruins of an ancient civilization and eat some really good food.

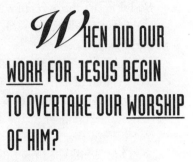

Where is Caesar today? Most of us know very little about Caesar—there's a salad named after him. Do we remember the names of the great emperors of Rome? For the most part, no.

When did our work for Jesus begin to overtake our worship of Him?

One of them, Diocletian, relentlessly persecuted the church, causing it to go underground. He thought he had been successful in obliterating Christians. He actually had a commemorative coin struck, with these words engraved on it: "The Christian religion is destroyed, and the worship of the Roman gods is restored."

Where is Diocletian today? Gone. Where are Christians today? Everywhere.

Over the centuries there have been many attempts to destroy the Christian faith. But they have always failed for one simple reason: Christians make up the body of Christ, which is the church. And Christ said that the gates of hell would not prevail against it. Jesus Christ will prevail in the end and establish His kingdom. But He'll do it His way through His people, His church.

You and the Church
One of the most important key to becoming part of God's upside-down church is caring about His church, both universally and locally.

The early apostles cared desperately about one another and

about all the Christian churches that were forming. They encouraged one another, wrote to one another, exhorted one another.

We have all heard this one: "Well, you know, I would go to church, but there are so many hypocrites there. I just can't stomach a hypocrite." I must say, what exactly are you looking for? A place filled with perfect people? Are you really shocked when you find that the church is filled with people just like you? People who are flawed, who make mistakes? Yes, even people who are sinners?

A lot of people are pretending to be something they aren't. The story is told of a man who was desperate to make some money. So he went down to the city zoo, hoping to get a job feeding the animals. The manager at the zoo had no openings, but seeing how big this guy was, he offered him another position.

"Our gorilla died the other day, and that was one of our most popular exhibits! If we got you a special gorilla suit, would you put it on and imitate him for a few days? We'll pay you well for it."

The guy was so desperate that he agreed. He actually did quite well at it for the next few days, dressed up in his gorilla suit, beating his chest, shaking the bars of his cage. Huge crowds were soon gathering, and the money was good.

But one day, while he was swinging on his trapeze, he lost his grip and landed right in the middle of the lion's den! The huge beast gave a ferocious roar. The man in the gorilla suit realized he couldn't cry for help without revealing that he was a fake. He slowly walked backwards away from the lion, hoping to climb back into his cage. The lion, however, with a very hungry look on his face, followed him.

Finally in desperation the gorilla cried, "Help!"

Immediately the lion whispered loudly, "Shut up, stupid, or you'll get us both fired!"

I have often said that if you are looking for the perfect church, don't join it because you'll spoil it. There is no church that does not have some flaws. The church is not supposed to be a museum for saints but a hospital for sinners. It's supposed to be a place where we can come and learn, grow, and help one another. And it's a place where we can go to be transformed.

Listen to what the Bible says in Hebrews 10:23-25:

> *Let us hold fast the confession of our hope without wavering, for He who promised is faithful. And let us consider one another in order to stir up love and good works, not forsaking the assembling of ourselves together, as is the manner of some, but exhorting one another, and so much the more as you see the Day approaching.* NKJV

The Bible is clearly saying that we should make time to be with other believers.

We are living in critical times. The Bible warns us that one of the signs of the last days will be an apostasy—a falling away from the faith: "Now the Holy Spirit tells us clearly that in the last times some will turn away from what we believe; they will follow lying spirits and teachings that come from demons" (1 Tim. 4:1, NLT).

If you are looking for the perfect church, don't join it because you'll spoil it.

We need to be together. We need to stand together. And when we face hardship, challenge, or temptation, we can come and be with God's people and say, "Pray for me this week. Help me." Or, we might be helpful to someone else.

Your Potential

Will you let Him fill you with His Holy Spirit? Will you value His purposes over people's priorities? Will you work according to His methods, not worldly ones?

If so, when God looks at you, He sees potential. You may see only a blank canvas, but He sees a finished painting. You see a Simon. He sees a Peter. You see a Gideon. He sees a mighty man of valor. God can do a lot with a little.

It's interesting to stop and look at how these men's lives ended. These were heroes of the faith. These were the few people who were faithful. And yet church tradition tells us that Matthew was slain with a sword. Luke was hung on an olive tree. James was beheaded. Philip was hanged. Andrew was bound to a cross from where he preached until he died. Thomas was thrust through with a spear. Simon Peter, the man who denied his Lord three times, was crucified upside down because he said, "I'm not worthy to die in the same way that my Lord died." That's not the same Peter I read about in the initial stages; that's a changed man.

John was the only apostle who was not martyred. Church tradition tells us that he was banished to the island of Patmos, where he was put into a pot of boiling oil—but John wouldn't cook. There on the island of Patmos he was given the message of the book of Revelation.

These were great men on whom God put His hand. Their greatness was not because of who they were; it was because of Christ, who lived in them and worked through them. God can make you into a great man or a great woman. Are you willing?

In the next chapter we'll look more closely at growing a healthy church, not just a large one. Believers who are world changers know that numbers are the result, not the goal, of the gospel. After all, in the days of the early church the Roman coliseums had the really big crowds. But across the empire, in marketplaces and jails and catacombs and rooms up back-alley stairs, something incredible was taking shape. Lives were changing. A new movement was being born.

The world was about to be tipped on its head.

And we can do the same today.

THREE

CONSUMERS OR COMMUNERS?

Church Growth Rules That
Could Be Making Yours Sick

THE CHURCH I pastor today actually began as a small Bible study over twenty-five years ago. Back then I had long hair parted down the middle, a full beard, and—well, you get the picture. Let's just say it was another place and time.

You see, I never expected to pastor a large church (I didn't even expect to pastor). We simply concentrated on learning and doing what Scripture teaches—and over time the Lord brought growth. We did not seek to be a big church; we sought to be a strong church. No one here at Harvest Fellowship gave size too much thought until a market research firm called one day and said, "Congratulations! You are one of the ten largest churches in America."

As a result of pastoring a large congregation, I'm frequently asked about our success. What kind of church growth formula do we follow? Can what we do at Harvest be applied to any church, anywhere, with similar results? In other words, "What's your secret fertilizer, and could we please have some?"

I understand these questions, and I know that the motivations behind them are often sincere. Very few pastors are interested in church growth solely to finance fat salaries or to feel more popular than they were in high school. But something would be terribly wrong if motivated Christians—pastors and laypeople alike—weren't interested in seeing their churches flourish and grow.

Over the years, some people have objected to our announcing how many people have become Christians in a particular service or rally at Harvest. They say, "You're not supposed to care about numbers." But why shouldn't we care about numbers?

Every number represents a soul. And I'm supposed to care about souls. So are you. The Bible tells us that the angels in heaven rejoice over every soul that is saved. We read in Acts that the early church kept count, too: "Then those who gladly received his word were baptized; and that day about three thousand souls were added to them" (Acts 2:41, NKJV).

It's quite possible to have a human body that's growing large—but not necessarily healthy.

We should do our best to get more people into church so more can hear the gospel, grow in Christ, and go out to multiply God's work in the world. This is our goal at Harvest Fellowship, and I believe it is the goal of almost every pastor I speak with.

So we agree that growth is good. Yet growth alone does not necessarily indicate that a church is healthy. When we see a church with high attendance, we can sometimes assume that the people there are doing some things right. But numbers don't tell the whole story.

Think of it this way. Paul told the Corinthians that the church is like a body with many different parts (1 Cor. 12:14-18). But as you know, it's quite possible to have a human body that's growing large—but not necessarily healthy. In fact, it's also possible for people to appear healthy even while their cholesterol count is off the charts or their liver is slowly disintegrating.

The simple truth is that size or growth rate alone does not indicate health. But health, on the other hand, almost always leads naturally to growth. This is particularly true when it comes to the church. That is why in this book we're focusing on health as a means to growth, not the other way around.

More and more pastors today are looking for ways to boost numbers. The past two decades have witnessed a dramatic increase in the number of "megachurches"—congregations of one thousand or more—around the country. Professionals have labeled the trend the "church growth movement."

But we have to ask what these trends mean for the church as a whole. Are we witnessing a second era of Christians who are really shaking up their world? Or are believers just shuffling their club memberships around to get the latest, most attractive deal?

I want us to look at how this new emphasis on growth is affecting today's church.

GROWTH OR HOAX?

Question: Isn't it a good sign that there are a lot of huge churches cropping up? Why doesn't this mean there are more Christians than ever?

Answer: In a recent article entitled "The Myth of Church Growth," published in *Current Thoughts and Trends,* David Dunlap cites some troubling statistics. For example, at the very time megachurches have sprouted across the landscape, the proportion of Americans who claim to be "born again" has remained a constant 32 percent.

According to Dunlap, growth isn't coming from conversions but from transfers; they account for up to 80 percent of all growth taking place today. He goes on to quote C. Peter Wagner, one of the leading spokesmen for the movement, who admits, "I don't think there is anything intrinsically wrong with the church growth principles we've developed . . . yet somehow they don't seem to work."

I would suggest that one reason they don't work is that they tend to approach church as if it were a business. But a business-driven response may only make things worse. In the long run, if we train people to be consumers instead of communers, we'll end up with customers instead of disciples. It might fill up an auditorium, but it'll never turn the world upside down for Christ.

The New Consumer Church

In my conversations with many pastors from around the country, I've noticed that a new word has entered church lingo: consumer.

If we train people to be consumers instead of communers, we'll end up with customers instead of disciples.

Experts are telling us that people no longer attend a fellowship of believers to commune with God. They come to consume. And in order to thrive, churches are going to have to adapt to the needs of the "spiritual consumer."

When you label someone a consumer, you're zeroing in on one thing: consumption. That means it's all about appetite—what goes down the hatch. And churches that adopt a consumer-oriented approach in order to bring in the crowd often look to marketing experts to help them find out what consumers are hungry for.

In the past a group of leaders and believers might pray and ask God to show them where to plant a new church. Today they're likely to add a few steps. They'll say, "Let's do a market survey, find out where the growth is, figure out the demographics. Let's ask our target population what they want in a church. Then let's deliver it."

To better understand this shift in thinking, imagine the church as a business. You, as a church leader, are the owner/operator. You are trying to meet the needs of church "consumers," and you must compete with other nearby providers for the same customer.

Suddenly your concerns would change, although the change may be unnoticeable at first. You'd spend a lot more time asking questions such as:

> *There's always a new church down the street that has some nifty new program or wide-screen TV that we don't.*

- What can I do to make my product more appealing and unique?
- How can I improve customer service?
- How can I adjust what we offer to meet and beat the competition?

This shift toward consumerism is being driven, directly or indirectly, not by pastors but by demands and expectations of church "customers."

"People expect a full-service church," one young pastor told me. "And there's always a new church down the street that has some nifty new program or wide-screen TV that we don't."

Listen to this: In a recent survey of a thousand church attendees, respondents were asked, "Why does the church exist?" Among laypersons polled, 89 percent said the church's purpose was "to take care of my family's and my spiritual needs." Only 11 percent said the purpose of the church is "to win the world for Jesus Christ."

The pastors from those same churches gave nearly the opposite answer. Only 10 percent said the church exists to meet the needs of members. The vast majority chose as the purpose of the church "to win the world for Christ."

Clearly the drive for a new way to do church is partly the result of a conflict of expectations between pastors and laypeople. The pastor is asking, "What will it take to get you plugged in to this church?" And people in the pew are answering, "Meet the needs of my family and make church a place we want to come to."

PASTOR TO PASTOR

Risky Rules for Growing

Could any of these church growth rules be making yours sick?

Risky Rule #1: If it brings people in, it pleases God.
Risky Rule #2: The less confrontational or overt the gospel message, the better.
Risky Rule #3: Feed a church what it seems to be hungry for.
Risky Rule #4: Target your church to a particular demographic group.

New Ways of Doing God's Business

Now would be a good time to pose the question What's so wrong with thinking of people as consumers and churches as marketers?

From a pastor's perspective I see many good reasons to consider church from a consumer's viewpoint. Frankly, I think it's better to be sensitive to what people want and need rather than ignore those needs for the sake of religious agendas, which has caused so many traditional churches to become irrelevant in today's culture.

Some good things are happening as a result of the church growth movement. Motivated believers are trying harder than ever to be relevant to people's real needs. Christians are finding new ways to reach out into their communities. And people who would never have showed up before are walking through church doors.

But I see dangers as well. If we let ourselves get trapped into relying solely on slick marketing ploys when it comes to doing God's business in this world, we've shifted the focus from the message of the gospel to the way we package it.

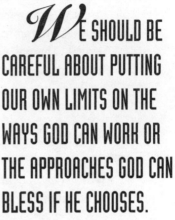

WE SHOULD BE CAREFUL ABOUT PUTTING OUR OWN LIMITS ON THE WAYS GOD CAN WORK OR THE APPROACHES GOD CAN BLESS IF HE CHOOSES.

The last thing I want to do is discourage any person or ministry or cause some unnecessary division. Christians are reaching for new ways of doing things because they see real needs in the world around us—and they care! I thank God for the diversity of church expressions in the body of Christ. And we should be careful about putting our own limits on the ways God can work or the approaches God can bless if He chooses.

But at the same time, we need to be aware of choices—even well-intentioned, highly attractive ones—that take our focus, time, and energy away from God's original plan for the church that we see reflected in the book of Acts.

MOVEMENTS VS. MARKETING

Question: Wasn't the Jesus movement of the late sixties and early seventies market driven in many ways? For instance, you did church on the beach and used guitars for worship. What's the difference between that and surfer churches or yuppie churches today?

Answer: I can't speak for the entire Jesus movement around the country at that time, only for what I was a part of at Calvary Chapel in Costa Mesa, California. The pastor of Calvary, Chuck Smith, allowed the young people to express themselves in the way and with the music that was a part of their culture. It was not at all contrived or even thought out. It was spontaneous. Looking back now, I believe it was a spiritual revival. There was a sense of expectancy in the air, a sense that God was truly at work.

Chuck had no master plan to speak of, just a desire to teach these young people the Word of God and help them mature spiritually. In fact, Chuck had built what for him was the ideal church sanctuary. It seated about three hundred in an intimate Spanish-style chapel. When the young kids starting showing up, they had to literally blow out walls to accommodate them. No surveys were taken, no market data analyzed.

God's Original Church Growth Plan

Recently I was at a gathering with some other pastors. Many of them were expressing frustration with the lack of numerical growth in their churches and were trying to figure out how to make their churches larger. One of them said, "My feeling is, whatever works, and if it pleases God, that is what I want to do."

I said, "You know, I don't want to be nitpicky, but I really have to correct that statement. It's not whatever works. It is whatever is pleasing to God. Period."

If it's pleasing to God, it will work.

God can meet the needs of our generation with or without a lot of spiffy marketing techniques to help Him out. At best they're optional. But what the church can never do without is God's own blueprints.

If there was ever a church growth plan that worked, it was the one used by the first-century church. Talk about numbers. Talk about effectiveness. This church exploded. Why? Because the believers knew why they were there and what they were supposed to do.

Eventually this little church scattered, divisions came, and persecution forced perseverance and, ultimately, growth. They certainly weren't perfect Christians or problem-free churches. However, when

> *I* BELIEVE THAT WHEN GOD SET UP THE FIRST CHURCH, HE DID IT RIGHT.

we talk about the upside-down church described in Acts, we're seeing the Original Plan in action. The apostles' letters to the churches complete the picture.

In the rest of this book I want to focus on that picture. What are the principles for "doing church" God's way? What should a world-changing body of believers really look and feel like? And what can we expect to see happen in our own congregations if we get it right?

In chapter 2, we quoted Acts 2:42-47, which describes the first church. In this passage we find four foundational qualities:

1. They were a worshiping church.
2. They were an evangelizing church.
3. They were a learning church.
4. They were a loving church.

Think of the word W-E-L-L: Worshiping, Evangelizing, Learning, and Loving. At a glance, these four foundations don't appear to be remarkable or, for that matter, upside down. They may not have the marquee appeal of a star-studded Sunday program.

But I believe that when God set up the first church, He did it right. Churches that try to consistently prioritize these areas the same way the first church did will discover two things: just how contrary to conventional wisdom they can run and how powerfully they work as a plan for church growth God's way.

Original Church Growth Rule #1:
Become a worshiping church.
"They continued steadfastly . . . in the breaking of bread, and in prayers. . . . And many wonders and signs were done through the apostles. . . . They ate their food with gladness and simplicity of heart, praising God."

*A*LTHOUGH PRAYER AND WORSHIP SOUND LIKE AUTOMATIC RESPONSES TO GOD'S MIRACLES, THEY OFTEN AREN'T.

The early church was built on prayer and worship. We might read this and think, *That's a no-brainer*, or *I'd worship and pray a lot too if I saw signs and wonders happening all around us.*

When we read the book of Acts—the record of the early church's history—we might conclude that the believers had miracles happen every single day! But we need to remember that Acts is an overview of about twenty-five years of church history. There were likely many days when miracles did not happen. But the believers continued on "steadfastly" because they did not follow signs and wonders. Rather, signs and wonders followed the believers.

Although prayer and worship sound like automatic responses to God's miracles, they often aren't. Actually, we see throughout the Gospels that a more common response is "Wow! Do that again, and I just might believe. In fact, if you keep providing this way, I might keep following you." But Jesus consistently refused to deliver to these consumers. King Herod wanted to see Jesus, so Jesus was brought before him. But the Bible says that what Herod really wanted was to see Jesus perform a miracle. Not only did Jesus not perform a miracle for Herod, He never even spoke to him (Luke 23:8-9). Herod was not interested in Christ himself or in His message; he just wanted to be dazzled.

When it comes to worship and prayer, one contemporary church growth rule seems to be: "Make your church a happening place. Lots of miracles. Lots of emotions. And people will come." I saw a notice permanently painted on a church sign the other day: "Miracle service every Wednesday night, 7 to 9." That amazed me. I just hope God knows when His window of opportunity is.

An expressive, worshipful church results from sincere praise and sincere communion with the Savior. It's not something you schedule in order to draw a crowd.

To become a worshiping people means that we've been turned upside down. Our natural inclination is to worship—with our time, energy, and affection—other gods. But the Bible teaches that we are put on this earth primarily to know and walk with the God who made us and to bring glory to His name.

Original Church Growth Rule #2:
Become an evangelistic church.
"The Lord added to the church daily those who were being saved."

As we read the accounts of the first church, it becomes clear that literally everything they did culminated in evangelism. Proclaiming Christ was never seen as optional. It was never a job handed out to a special committee. Evangelism happened regularly as the early believers lived their lives upside down in every way. As they did so, they aroused not only curiosity but also admiration and earned an audience with unbelievers.

Healthy, well-fed, worshiping believers will reproduce themselves.

Today, many in the church actually debate Jesus' command to go into all the world and make disciples for Him. Some churches go so far as to say, "We're not called to evangelism. We are called to body ministry." Or,

"We're called to get into the Word together. There are other churches called to outreach."

Healthy, well-fed, worshiping believers will reproduce themselves. When I am glorifying God, when I am built up as a believer, I want to then go and share my faith.

One positive aspect of the recent growth movement is the emphasis on getting unbelievers to join us at church. More churches are trying to make their service sensitive to the needs of unbelievers. Cut out the Christian jargon. Don't actually preach from a Bible, just refer to it. Make visitors feel welcome—no pressure, no appeals.

This is a great goal, and it has brought thousands of people into the church who would never have attended otherwise. The result has been a growing awareness of our need to abandon Christian jargon and communicate the gospel clearly. In some cases it's pulled us out of our cliques and clubs and forced us to relate to unbelievers.

CREATIVE APPROACHES SHOULD WORK TO STRENGTHEN THE GOSPEL'S IMPACT, NOT OBSCURE IT.

However, I believe there is a potential downside. Sometimes a church tries so hard not to be offensive or confrontational that the gospel message is not preached in its entirety. I'm totally in favor of meeting people with Christ's message in creative ways. But this should work to strengthen the gospel's impact, not obscure it. If people walk away having a good feeling but no idea who Jesus is, we've really missed the boat.

This does not mean that drama is wrong or that using videos, music, or any other means to communicate the gospel is wrong. We do some of those things at Harvest. But it does mean that we must be sure that gimmicks don't take the place of the gospel, and that we are actually proclaiming the whole gospel—including judgment, sin, and salvation.

Paul put it this way, "How, then, can they call on the one they have not believed in? And how can they believe in the one of whom they have not heard? And how can they hear without someone preaching to them?" (Rom. 10:14, NIV).

We must realize that God's primary method of converting people is through biblical preaching. Scripture reminds us, "For since in the wisdom of God the world through its wisdom did not know him, God was pleased through the foolishness of [the message] preached to save those who believe" (1 Cor. 1:21, NKJV).

Notice that the verse does not say people would be saved by foolish preaching, though there is plenty of that. Nor does it say that people would be saved by the foolishness of Christian music, as wonderful as that can be, or by the foolishness of drama and skits. But rather, through the foolishness of *the message preached.*

I do believe that we make a grave mistake when we discourage people from bringing their Bibles to church. George Barna's book *The Second Coming of the Church* mentions that in the seventies, seeker churches wanted to make visitors feel welcome. So they did not make it necessary for people to locate Bibles or find passages in them. Churches didn't want visitors to feel that they were surrounded by what could be perceived as a bunch of "Bible thumpers." Barna says, "Two decades later, it is clear that this experiment has had a more sinister consequence. People don't even know where their Bibles are anymore!" In many churches, the core membership—not just the visitors for whom the tactic was originally embraced, has lost its familiarity with the Bible. He concluded, "Sadly, the shift away from promoting the personal responsibility to bring a Bible along has sent a signal to many people that the Bible is not important."

Original Church Growth Rule #3: Become a learning church.
"They continued steadfastly in the apostles' doctrine and fellowship."

This most basic essential of any healthy church is a commitment to preaching and learning God's Word. At the time of the first church, this meant listening to the apostles' teachings and reading the Scripture they had at this point.

But also notice the words "they continued steadfastly." Keep in mind that this means not only that the apostles taught faithfully and continually but that the congregation was faithful to "continue in"—learn and keep growing in—what was taught. They were attentive.

This may not appear to be upside-down behavior. But if you continue to follow the story of the first church, you see how the more common approach was to neglect sound teaching or to change the gospel's message. Paul wrote to the churches in Galatia:

> *I am astonished that you are so quickly deserting the one who called you by the grace of Christ and are turning to a different gospel—which is really no gospel at all. Evidently some people are throwing you into confusion and are trying to pervert the gospel of Christ.* Gal. 1:6-7, NIV

I do believe that in some churches the Bible is simply not being preached and taught with a view to giving the congregation a deepening understanding of Scripture.

It's true that many people today want church "lite" and hassle free. No heavy meals or five-course messages. They want to just drive in, place their order, and drive out.

But the danger here is that people develop an appetite for what they are fed. A church with a steady diet of feel-good sermonettes in place of good theology or solid teaching from Scripture will eventually raise up a congregation that is weak.

The writer of Hebrews expressed it this way:

We have much to say about this, but it is hard to explain because you are slow to learn. In fact, though by this time you ought to be teachers, you need someone to teach you the elementary truths of God's word all over again. You need milk, not solid food! Anyone who lives on milk, being still an infant, is not acquainted with the teaching about righteousness. But solid food is for the mature, who by constant use have trained themselves to distinguish good from evil. Heb. 5:11-14, NIV

Original Church Growth Rule #4: Become a loving church. "Now all who believed were together, and had all things in common . . . continuing daily with one accord . . . and having favor with all the people."

Having all things in common. This is definitely upside down, and it's hard for many of us to even picture it. Of course, others of us think it sounds great: "Hey, the Carlson's would have to share their boat with us. . . ."

But this description wasn't intended to describe some socialist plot. It illustrates just how literally we're called to love one another. The reason the early church could share their possessions was that they were actually living out the second great command to love their neighbor as themselves. We see that their unity and love were so powerful that "all the people" thought well of them.

Who wouldn't want to join in on such a love fest where everyone was cared about and accepted? As a result, their numbers exploded and thousands came to Christ.

I think most people would agree that today the church at large doesn't live out this kind of unity or love. Many local congregations struggle to keep their own church from splitting in two. And meanwhile various church denominations squabble and spit at each other across the aisles while the world looks on. We seem to have forgotten that our commitment to love and unity in the church is one of the most powerful ways we witness to the world. And this is tragic.

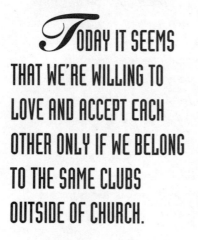

Today it seems that we're willing to love and accept each other only if we belong to the same clubs outside of church. One of the latest trends in church growth is the attempt to try to "niche" churches in a particular segment of society. You might call them designer churches. "Let's have boomers," or "Let's get the Generation Xers."

There's nothing wrong with trying to make a connection with a specific segment of society. Or choosing common interests as springboards to evangelization. We naturally invite to church our friends and others who share our interests.

But the problem with designing a church to cater specifically only to a certain group of people is that we miss out on the great beauties of diversity.

Jesus said, "Go into all the world, and preach the gospel." He did not say, "Go only to the people you can personally relate to" or "Pick a particular demographic group, and then go love them." Paul wrote to the Colossians, "So, naturally, we proclaim Christ! We warn everyone we meet, and we teach everyone we can, all that we know about him" (Col. 1:28, Phillips).

I think it's wonderful when someone walks into the church and sees different ages, different cultures, different tastes, different races—with one thing in common: Jesus Christ. That is a truly loving church. And that church will grow.

Beyond Formulas

The acronym I've used here—W-E-L-L—is simply a way to remember these four key principles. But the foundations of the first church are not just another formula. They are God's original design for a healthy, growing church. Throughout the rest of this book we will be focusing on how to live upside-down lives and create upside-down churches, based on these four key areas.

Yet while every church and every Christian's life should be built on these four foundations, each one should go about this differently. Your goal should not be to have a church that looks just like mine or anyone else's. Your goal should be to become part of a healthy, balanced, diverse church that is bringing souls into God's kingdom.

I believe that the church in our generation has a unique opportunity to make a difference in the world. God has opened the doors wide to us at this time in history, and we can use this opportunity to get the gospel out and to turn the world upside down.

We shouldn't think, however, that this is the first time the church has been tempted to treat itself like a gathering of consumers instead of communers. Remember Jesus' outrage at the marketplace? "Then he entered the temple area and began driving out those who were selling. 'It is written,' he said to them, '"My house will be a house of prayer"; but you have made it "a den of robbers"'" (Luke 19:45-46, NIV).

Every one of us has a vital part to play in helping our house of prayer grow healthy. But as we do, let's remember that God's church is not a business. It may grow larger when it's treated like one. But what will be the long-term prognosis? God's church is based on principles that go against the world's grain. So healthy growth cannot come from applying worldly methods.

FOUR

"GO THEREFORE..."
God's Upside-Down Plan to Save the World

FEW THINGS in the Bible are more upside down than God's plan to save the world. Think about this for a moment. The all-powerful God of the universe chose limited, fallible human beings as His main vehicle to spread the most important message the world has ever known.

He could have chosen angels to do the job. He could have parted the clouds and spoken audibly and said something like, "Hello, humanity. I'm God and you're not!"

In the past He spoke through a burning bush, appeared in visions, and carved His laws on stone tablets. But in our day He has clearly chosen ordinary men and women to carry His message of salvation to the world.

The Great Commission
If you've been a Christian for long, you've probably heard of the great commission. Some of you can't hear the words without worrying that God will send you to Siberia as a missionary. Or maybe you're not familiar with the term at all, and you're thinking, *The great commission . . . is that some kind of spiritual kickback we get every time we lead someone to Christ?*

Well, yes and no. I know of nothing in life so rewarding as

leading people to Christ. But technically the great commission refers to Jesus' command in Matthew 28:18-20:

> *Jesus came and spoke to them, saying, "All authority has been given to Me in heaven and on earth. Go therefore and make disciples of all the nations, baptizing them in the name of the Father and of the Son and of the Holy Spirit, teaching them to observe all things that I have commanded you; and lo, I am with you always, even to the end of the age."* NKJV

It's important to note that although Jesus was speaking to His disciples here, this commission is intended for the entire church—not just pastors, evangelists, and missionaries. And the great commission is not something Jesus said only once. It's emphasized many times throughout the New Testament.

Remember the parable of the virgins, or bridesmaids, found in Matthew 25? In this story about a first-century wedding, when a shout indicated that the bridegroom had arrived to escort the bride to the wedding, five bridesmaids had enough oil in their lamps and were ready to go. But five were foolish and said, "We don't have enough oil in our lamps. Can you give us some of yours?" The wise ones essentially answered, "Sorry, go get it for yourself." The door was shut, and they never got in.

THE GREAT COMMISSION IS INTENDED FOR THE ENTIRE CHURCH—NOT JUST PASTORS, EVANGELISTS, AND MISSIONARIES.

Clearly this parable is a warning from Jesus to the "pseudobeliever" (who is really not a believer at all) who sits in the pew every Sunday but has no real relationship with God. The oil Jesus mentioned in this story could be taken to symbolize the Holy Spirit in the believer's life. These five virgins

58

without oil are a picture of those who may outwardly appear to be Christian but really aren't. Most messages I have heard on this text tend to emphasize that aspect of the parable, and I have given more than one message myself doing that very thing.

But something else strikes me about this story, something that speaks to true Christians also. Notice that those who had oil had no plan to give some to those who didn't: "Then the five foolish ones asked the others, 'Please give us some of your oil because our lamps are going out.' But the others replied, 'We don't have enough for all of us. Go to a shop and buy some for yourselves'" (Matt. 25:8-9, NLT). Our attitude as Christians can easily slip into "I got mine. You go get yours. I'm going to heaven—too bad you're not."

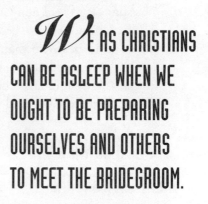
WE AS CHRISTIANS CAN BE ASLEEP WHEN WE OUGHT TO BE PREPARING OURSELVES AND OTHERS TO MEET THE BRIDEGROOM.

Notice, too, that when the cry went out to announce the bridegroom's arrival, both the wise and the foolish were sleeping. I think that is an important point. It clearly shows that we as Christians can be asleep when we ought to be preparing ourselves and others to meet the Bridegroom.

Jesus also told a story about a shepherd who had one hundred sheep. One went astray. The shepherd didn't say, "Win a few, lose a few." He left the ninety-nine. He went after that one sheep. Why? Because God doesn't value just multitudes; He values individuals. He values humans. He values the human soul.

We saw in chapter 3 that evangelism was one of the four foundations of the first church. But as we read about the early church in Acts, we notice that whether we're talking about learning, loving, or worshiping, all these things are ultimately part of making the church more equipped for evangelism. We might call "the equipping of the saints" our marching orders.

So how is the church responding?

The Great Concession

Some time ago *Christianity Today* magazine conducted a survey among its readers and found that most of them, 89 percent, agreed that faith in Jesus Christ was the only way to salvation. And 87 percent of the readers agreed that every Christian is responsible for evangelism. But only 68 percent of the respondents agreed or strongly agreed that the most important task for Christians is to lead non-Christians to faith in Christ. And only 52 percent said, "I have been more active in telling others about Christ in the past year than ever before."

I think these findings are fairly representative of the rank-and-file Christians in today's church. Most of us know that Christ is the only way to God. And we realize that evangelism is part of our calling, yet we respond to the great commission with something like, "Oh yeah, we're supposed to go tell every nation. . . . I'm pretty sure part of my offering goes to one of those missions groups."

So how did the great commission become the great concession?

The readers responding to the *Christianity Today* survey named a number of problems, including: (1) A feeling that I am not able to do evangelism as well as the professional; (2) I'm too timid; (3) I fear how people will respond. These feelings are very real, and in the next chapter we address some of them. But I believe the biggest reason we in the church are not carrying out the great commission is that we don't care enough. We're simply not that concerned about the souls of others.

General William Booth, the founder of the Salvation Army, once said that if he could have his wish, part of the final training for preachers and evangelists would be to have them hung over the open fires of hell for twenty-four hours "so those that were sharing this gospel message would recognize the urgency of it," he explained.

The early church understood this urgency. Paul put it this way to the church at Corinth:

> *We are therefore Christ's ambassadors, as though God were making his appeal through us. We implore you on Christ's behalf: Be reconciled to God. God made him who had no sin to be sin for us, so that in him we might become the righteousness of God.* 2 Cor. 5:20-21, NIV

Notice that God is making His "appeal" through us. And Christ is "imploring" unbelievers through us. The God of the universe is pleading with fallen humanity through us. If this doesn't inspire us, I don't know what will.

The first church was persecuted for preaching, and yet listen to this:

> *They called the apostles in and had them flogged. Then they ordered them not to speak in the name of Jesus, and let them go. The apostles left the Sanhedrin, rejoicing because they had been counted worthy of suffering disgrace for the Name. Day after day, in the temple courts and from house to house, they never stopped teaching and proclaiming the good news that Jesus is the Christ.* Acts 5:40-42, NIV

Did you catch that? This is definitely upside-down behavior: rejoicing because they suffered. Here in the U.S. there's not much sales appeal for that kind of attitude. We have the opportunity to proclaim Christ without serious persecution for the most part. Yet the church is often casual about it.

In sharp contrast, these early Christians continued to do the very thing that had caused them to suffer. If I saw men behaving like this, it would get my attention. I'd want to know exactly what cause or person they believed in so passionately.

Meet a man named Andrew Meekin.

You may remember reading about the jet that was hijacked, then crashed with 163 passengers and 12 crew members on board. As it turned out, these hijackers bungled their plans, and there was not enough fuel to get to their destination. So the pilot announced to the passengers that he was going to have to do an emergency landing on water.

*T*HESE EARLY CHRISTIANS CONTINUED TO DO THE VERY THING THAT HAD CAUSED THEM TO SUFFER.

Enter Andrew Meekin, a man on his way to a Bible conference. Andrew was a member of the evangelical church in Ethiopia, in Addis Ababa, the capital. Even though he was a soft-spoken man and not a preacher per se, when he heard that the plane was going to make an emergency landing, he stood up. In the final anxious minutes between that announcement and the crash, Andrew Meekin quickly shared the gospel message with the passengers and invited people to respond. A flight attendant who survived said that twenty people received Christ.

Andrew Meekin seized his opportunity. And I know what you're thinking: *OK, next time I'm on a plane that's going down I'll do that. I think under those circumstances, I'd feel urgent, too.* We probably would. But the Christian who is living according to Christ's upside-down principles believes and acts as if the plane could always go down. He is prepared and poised to seize the moment.

Be honest with yourself. Measure your response by your behavior and your choices, not by your feelings or intentions: Do you really care about the plight of the unbeliever? Every unbelieving person you meet today is in danger of dying without Christ at any moment.

I know these words are hard. So let me encourage you that if you're becoming painfully aware that you don't care enough about lost souls, that in itself is a good indication that you do care. I know that many believers fall into bed at night discouraged. Many of us are embarrassed that we've never led others to Christ. And we're not sure why, but it seems that our Christian walk lacks results. May I suggest to you that the answer is simple. It's as simple as asking God to wake you up. As being willing to take steps of faith and try to initiate conversations about Christ. It's as simple as asking God to give you a sincere burden for the lost. It's as simple as looking around every day to see what part you can play in God's amazing plan of redemption.

*W*INNERS OF SOULS MUST FIRST BE WEEPERS OF SOULS.

PASTOR TO PASTOR
"Weepers of Souls"

Some time ago I was asked to speak to a group of pastors on the subject of church growth and evangelism. I told these pastors that the reason many of their churches were not growing was that many of them really didn't care about evangelizing lost people.

Later, one pastor wrote me a letter saying, "My first reaction to your message was, 'How dare you say to me, a pastor, a man of God, that I don't care about lost people?' But then I began to think about it. I began to pray about it. And I realized you were right. I cared about my flock and our own ministry but not the lost.

"So I asked God to give me a burden, and He changed my heart. Now we are inviting unbelievers to Christ in our services, and every week people put their faith in Jesus."

We can talk endlessly about the need for evangelism. And we can create programs designed to mobilize our church with resources and tools. But it is of no consequence if the body of Christ doesn't care. We've got to start on the inside and work out.

It was C. H. Spurgeon who said, "Winners of souls must first be weepers of souls." And I would add that pastors must be weepers of souls if we want our congregations to become winners of souls.

Ask yourself with me, "When was the last time I wept because people need Christ?"

A Part to Play: Our Role in the Great Commission

The great commission is a joint effort.

When you think of your own conversion, you will remember that, yes, there was a moment when it all came into focus and you made that commitment to Christ. But probably a series of things brought you to that decision. It might have been the foundation your parents laid or a talk you had with a friend. It might have been something you were exposed to on TV or radio.

We all have a part to play. Some of us break down an intellectual barrier. Some of us come along and penetrate a heart's stubborn defenses with our own story about what Christ has done for us. Others of us sense when someone is ready, and we're led to actually pray with a person to receive Christ.

The apostle Paul put it this way in 1 Corinthians 3:6-8:

> *I planted the seed, Apollos [another preacher] watered it, but God made it grow. So neither he who plants nor he who waters is anything, but only God, who makes things grow. The man who plants and the man who waters have one purpose, and each will be rewarded according to his own labor.* NIV

Meet another guy, Edward Kimball. He sold shoes. But that's not how he changed the world.

Edward Kimball was an ordinary Christian who taught Sunday school in his church and made a living down at the shoe store. But his real passion was sharing the gospel. One day Edward determined that he was going to look for an opportunity to explain the gospel to a salesman named Dwight, who had just joined the staff.

Edward was really nervous. He hemmed and hawed and paced back and forth. Dwight was in the back room putting shoes away. Finally Edward mustered up his courage and launched into the story of Jesus' birth and death and resurrection. That day young Dwight gave his life to Christ.

Maybe you've already guessed. Dwight's last name was Moody. You may know him as D. L. Moody. So Edward Kimball, a shoe salesman, led to Christ one who would be one of the greatest evangelists in church history. This is the great commission in action. It's not just about what pastors and evangelists do from the pulpit. It's about what you do and say while you're selling shoes or programming computers or shuttling neighbor kids to soccer practice.

If the story stopped here, that would be amazing. But it continues. One day Dwight L. Moody was preaching, and a pastor named Frederick Meyer was listening. He was deeply stirred by Moody's message and went on to establish a nationwide preaching ministry. Later, while he was preaching, a young man in the audience named Wilbur Chapman accepted Christ.

Eventually Chapman felt called to evangelism. As he was proclaiming the gospel in various places, he decided he needed some help. He knew a young former baseball player named Billy Sunday, who was looking for a job, and Chapman hired him. Billy asked if he could preach every now and then. Billy Sunday ultimately emerged as the greatest preacher of the early 1900s.

One day Billy Sunday preached in Charlotte, North Carolina, where a great movement of God was taking place. Many people believed. They were so stirred up in their new faith that they invited a relatively unknown preacher, Mordecai Ham, to set up his gospel tent in Charlotte and keep preaching. On one of the final nights a tall, lanky farm boy walked down the aisle. His name was Billy Frank, but more of us know him today as Billy Graham. And he has personally delivered the gospel message to more people than any other man in human history.

IT'S WORTH NOTING THAT NO PERSON IN THE NEW TESTAMENT CAME TO FAITH APART FROM THE AGENCY OF A HUMAN BEING.

Think about that. Edward Kimball reached D. L. Moody, who reached F. B. Meyer, who reached Wilbur Chapman, who touched Billy Sunday, who touched those who brought Mordecai Ham to town to preach the gospel to Billy Graham.

We don't always celebrate the Andrew Meekins and Edward Kimballs of the world. We remember the D. L. Moodys and the Billy Sundays and the Billy Grahams. But God has placed His faithful ones everywhere. And we all have a crucial part to play.

It's worth noting that no person in the New Testament came to faith apart from the agency of a human being. Why didn't the angel of the Lord just go straight to the Ethiopian and skip Philip? And what about Cornelius? He was commanded by an angel to send for Simon Peter, who "will tell you what you must do" (Acts 10:6, NKJV). Why didn't the angel just tell him?

Because God has chosen to work through people. Even in the unique case of Saul of Tarsus, a person prepared the way. Before Stephen was stoned, as Saul stood by, approving, Stephen fearlessly proclaimed the gospel message. And then after Saul encountered the Lord on the road to Damascus, God sent a man named Ananias to lay hands on him and pray for him.

Does this mean that God can't save the world without people? Is God actually dependent on us? No. God can get the job done without you or me. But in His wisdom God has chosen people to communicate His message. And although God could get the job done without us, we could never get the job done without Him.

A Mission Possible: God's Role in the Great Commission

God's role in the great commission is greater than you may realize, because even though God gave this assignment to humans, He didn't leave it at that. When He commissioned us, He also committed Himself to helping us.

You'll notice that the word *commission* doesn't appear in Matthew 28. My thesaurus lists the synonyms *entrust, authorize, empower*. And each one of these is reflected in the words of Jesus and helps us understand God's part in the great commission.

GOD ENTRUSTS US. Have you ever had to entrust someone with an important message? You hope they get it right. You pray it gets delivered. Above all, you want the messenger to value the message as much you do. Just before Jesus announced the great commission, "the eleven disciples went to Galilee, to the mountain where Jesus had told them to go. When they saw him, they worshiped him; but some doubted. Then Jesus came to them and said . . ." (Matt. 28:16-18, NIV).

In His next words to the disciples, Jesus entrusted them with the most important message in the world. He gave them the great commission— *even while some were still doubting!*

Jesus didn't give the command only to those who firmly believed or had a special gift for talking to people. He gave it to all of them. He chose to trust this group with His appeal. Even if we have fears or doubts, we are still called. God has chosen to trust us with this precious mission.

JESUS GAVE THEM THE GREAT COMMISSION— EVEN WHILE SOME WERE STILL DOUBTING!

HE AUTHORIZES US. Notice these words in the great commission: "All authority . . . has been given to me." Jesus was saying two things here. The first was: "I have total authority and control here. I am in charge of everyone and everything. You can't appeal to a higher power. And so you can rest assured that this assignment comes from the top."

Those of you with a military background understand this concept well. Your superior officer has the authority to tell you what to do. And when he speaks, you jump. Others of us can remember a baby-sitter who used this line on us. She said, "I'm in charge now. Remember that your parents have given me all authority. You have to do what I say." And we knew she was right.

Listen to Paul describing to the Colossians our authority through Jesus:

> For by him all things were created: things in heaven and on earth, visible and invisible, whether thrones or powers or rulers or authorities; all things were created by him and for him. He is before all things, and in him all things hold together. And he is the head of the body, the church; he is the beginning and the firstborn from among the dead, so that in everything he might have the supremacy.
> Col. 1:16-18, NIV

The second aspect of what Jesus is saying is this: When someone with ultimate authority has sent us to do something, we suddenly have authority ourselves. We read in Matthew 10:1 that before Jesus sent them out, "he called his twelve disciples to him and gave them authority to drive out evil spirits and to heal every disease and sickness" (NIV).

Think about a time when you had to accomplish a particular task at work. You went to a coworker and said, "I need thus and so."

And he or she said, "Hmmm, I'll think about it."

But then you piped up and said, "The boss sent me. And he needs this by 2:00 P.M."

"Oh. OK. I'll have it ready, no problem."

The great commission is not just something God told us to go out and do apart from him. He backs us up. He is our authority, and He lends us His authority as we go out into the world to do His will.

HE EMPOWERS US. Let's go back for a moment to the military analogy. You've been entrusted with an important message. And now you've been given authority to deliver it. But what if you have no means? "That's great, Sarge, but don't I get any backup? How am I supposed to accomplish this?"

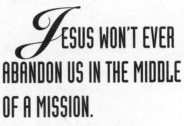

JESUS WON'T EVER ABANDON US IN THE MIDDLE OF A MISSION.

We all know what it's like to be asked to do a task that seems impossible, either because we don't know how to do the job or we don't have the resources we need. We may feel this way about evangelizing. *How can I ever get brave enough? What do I say?*

But the great news is that when God commissions us, He also empowers us to be His witnesses.

After the great commission in Matthew, we read in the book of Acts how Jesus appeared to the disciples yet again and said,

> *Do not leave Jerusalem, but wait for the gift my Father promised, which you have heard me speak about. For John baptized with water, but in a few days you will be baptized with the Holy Spirit. . . . You will receive power when the Holy Spirit comes on you; and you will be my witnesses in Jerusalem, and in all Judea and Samaria, and to the ends of the earth.* Acts 1:4-8, NIV

Basically God is saying here, "Wait! Don't think you can just go out and do this on your own. You need special power; you need my very Spirit within you."

A. W. Tozer said that if the Holy Spirit were taken away from the New Testament church, 90 percent of what they did would come to a halt, but if the Holy Spirit were taken away from the church of today, 10 percent of what we do would come to a halt.

Jesus promises to personally empower us. And He won't ever abandon us in the middle of a mission.

A FIRE IN THE PULPIT

Question: How can I be sure my congregation is really getting the message of the great commission? What can a pastor really do to set his congregation on fire?

Answer: It's been said, "The best way to get a fire in the pews is to first start one in the pulpit."

If you are a pastor or a Bible study leader, your heart and attitude will show themselves in what you say and how you say it. It was Moody who reminded us that we should never preach about hell without a tear in our eye or about heaven without a smile on our face.

Your people need to see that the plight of lost men and women is important to *you*. Reinforce the need to share the gospel often by teaching what Scripture says about responsibility. Perhaps the most important thing you can do is to be sure that you are consistently obeying the commission yourself by offering—from the pulpit—invitations for people to follow Christ.

When the people you speak to hear this kind of emphasis, it will remind them of the importance of seeking to lead others to Christ.

FIVE

DO YOU KNOW JESUS?
Practical Principles
for Witnessing

THE FIRST time I led someone to Jesus Christ, I did not expect the gospel to work. Not through my mouth anyway. My only plan was to fail.

I was two weeks old in my commitment to Christ. I didn't know much about Christian living or the Bible, but I'd heard that I should go out and share the Good News with others. So one day I went down to the beach—the same one where I used to make a point of avoiding any Bible-toting Christians who might try to witness to me.

Now here I was, a bona fide member of the Soul Patrol, out prowling for unbelievers to convert. But I wasn't exactly full of confidence. My main goal was to find someone who wouldn't argue or get angry at me. I thought if an unbeliever just ignored me or walked away, that would be fine.

Eventually I spotted a lady who looked about the age of my mom. I imagined that she might be sympathetic to me. When I walked up to her, my voice was shaking. I said, "Excuse me, but can I talk to you or something?"

She said, "Sure. What about?"

"Uh, about, like, God and stuff." (Remember, I was a teenager.) She said, "Go ahead. Sit down. Talk to me."

So I pulled out a copy of an evangelistic tract I had stuffed in my pocket for a moment like this. Since I couldn't remember exactly what it said in there, I read through the entire booklet verbatim. The whole time I read, I was shaking like a leaf and thinking, *This isn't going to work. Why am I doing this? This is not going to reach her.*

But the woman didn't leave.

When I got to a part that said, "Is there any good reason why you should not accept Jesus Christ right now?" I realized that I should direct this question to the woman. I hesitated. Feeling awkward, I looked up and asked her, "Is there?"

She said, "No."

"OK," I said, slightly confused. "Then that would mean you would like to accept Jesus Christ right now?"

She said, "Yes, I would."

I was so shocked that for a moment I didn't know what to do. I had planned only for failure. Frantically I searched the tract for some kind of prayer to lead her in. Finding one, I said in the most reverent tone I could summon, "Let's bow our heads for a word of prayer." But even as she prayed after me, I was still thinking, *This is not going to work!*

After we were done, the woman looked up and said, "Something just happened to me." And at that moment, something happened to me, too. I got a taste of what it was like to be used by God.

I had completely underestimated the power of the gospel. But I determined that from that point on, no matter what else I did in life, I wanted to share my faith with others.

It's Time to Hit the Beach

By now you understand that the great commission applies to everyone in the body of Christ. And I hope you've asked God to give you and your church a burning desire to see people come into God's kingdom. Now it's time to actually hit the beach. Or the streets. Or wherever it is you or your congregation meets unbelievers.

In this chapter we'll look at the practical aspects of how to actually approach unbelievers and be effective witnesses for Christ.

Remember the *Christianity Today* survey I mentioned in chapter 4? The reasons most Christians listed for not witnessing were: (1) A feeling that I am not able to do evangelism as well as the professional; (2) I'm too timid; (3) I fear how people will respond.

I HAD COMPLETELY UNDERESTIMATED THE POWER OF THE GOSPEL.

One thing Christians and non-Christians have in common is that they're both uptight about evangelism. Christians are uptight about witnessing to unbelievers, and unbelievers are uptight about being witnessed to by Christians. I can relate to both sides. Before I met the Lord, I was definitely the person on the beach you'd least want to pick on. I became pretty skilled at hanging out that Do Not Disturb sign to any would-be evangelists.

When you think about it, witnessing is sort of an upside-down thing to do. It goes against our natural avoidance of rejection or telling people something they may not want to hear. The idea doesn't exactly appeal to the church's new consumer mentality. Add to this the deep terror many of us feel about the idea of speaking in public, and you have a lot of reasons to stay home and keep your faith to yourself.

I have seen surveys taken where people are asked to identify their greatest fears. The predictable responses are these: fear of flying, spiders, being audited by the IRS, etc. But what always amazes me is that the number one fear is not death (that's number two) but rather having to speak publicly.

You may have heard the story from the days of the Roman

Empire about a Christian who was thrown to a hungry lion in the Colosseum. As the bloodthirsty spectators cheered, the lion pounced on the Christian. But the Christian quickly whispered something in the lion's ear, and the beast backed away in terror. After this happened several times, the emperor sent a centurion to find out what magic spell could make a ferocious lion cower in fear. A few minutes later the guard returned and said, "The Christian told the lion, 'After dinner you'll be required to say a few words.'"

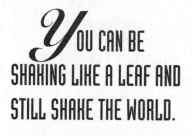

YOU CAN BE SHAKING LIKE A LEAF AND STILL SHAKE THE WORLD.

Yes, witnessing can seem scary. But the lessons I learned that day at the beach still hold true. For those willing to risk a little personal rejection, the rewards go way beyond any awkward moments they might experience. And any Christian—no matter how young in the faith or terror-stricken or awkward or doubting—can learn how to effectively lead an unbeliever to Christ.

I know firsthand that it doesn't take a lot of training for someone to be able to proclaim the gospel. The story proves this point. And have you noticed that often the most effective evangelists in a church are usually the youngest Christians? They have no idea that they might not be up to the task. Their passion and sincerity more than make up for any lack of knowledge or training.

However, I don't believe that hoping all the baby Christians will witness is a good plan for turning the world on its ear. Let's face it. As the church has responded to the great commission with a great concession, few are taking the time to say, "You need to do this—and here's how." I'm always amazed at the number of pastors and church workers who admit they haven't trained their people to witness with any kind of confidence.

What I'm about to show you won't necessarily make evangelism easy for you or your congregation. Some people will always feel uncomfortable proclaiming the gospel. But you know what? It doesn't have to be comfortable. In fact, I know this from experience: *You can be shaking like a leaf and still shake the world.*

PASTOR TO PASTOR
A Message Worth Repeating

You might be surprised to learn that many pastors feel as awkward preaching the gospel from the pulpit as their laypeople do sharing it on the job. In fact, some consider it unseemly to preach the gospel from the pulpit.

It's much more comfortable to preach about some other aspect of Christian living, such as fellowship or kindness. Everybody pretty much agrees with these things. But the true gospel message is inherently confrontational. In fact, some pastors have had complaints from their congregation when they have tried to accurately present the gospel from the pulpit. One pastor said, "Every time I preach about repentance and give an invitation, I can see my congregation squirm." Other pastors find that the gospel message doesn't measure up to their loftier themes and sounds slightly ridiculous.

I don't always succeed, but I try, in most messages I give, to present a simple gospel message and include at the end an invitation for people to come to Jesus. I believe that if there's a single thing I do as a pastor that has contributed to my church's growth and health, this is probably it.

For not only is it an opportunity to "throw out the net" and give people a chance to receive Christ, but it also models for the congregation how the gospel should be presented: simply and sincerely.

Salvation in the Desert

We find the story of Philip in Acts 8.

> *Now an angel of the Lord spoke to Philip, saying, "Arise and go toward the south along the road which goes down from Jerusalem to Gaza." This is desert. So he arose and went. And behold, a man of Ethiopia, a eunuch of great authority under Candace the queen of the Ethiopians, who had charge of all her treasury, and had come to Jerusalem to worship, was returning. And sitting in his chariot, he was reading Isaiah the prophet. Then the Spirit said to Philip, "Go near and overtake this chariot."*
>
> *So Philip ran to him, and heard him reading the prophet Isaiah, and said, "Do you understand what you are reading?"*
>
> *And he said, "How can I, unless someone guides me?" And he asked Philip to come up and sit with him. The place in the Scripture which he read was this: "He was led as a sheep to the slaughter; and as a lamb before its shearer is silent, so He opened not His mouth. In His humiliation His justice was taken away, and who will declare His generation? For His life is taken from the earth."*
>
> *So the eunuch answered Philip and said, "I ask you, of whom does the prophet say this, of himself or of some other man?" Then Philip opened his mouth, and beginning at this Scripture, preached Jesus to him. Now as they went down the road, they came to some water. And the eunuch said, "See, here is water. What hinders me from being baptized?"*
>
> *Then Philip said, "If you believe with all your heart, you may."*
>
> *And he answered and said, "I believe that Jesus Christ is the Son of God."*
>
> *So he commanded the chariot to stand still. And both*

Philip and the eunuch went down into the water, and
he baptized him. Now when they came up out of the
water, the Spirit of the Lord caught Philip away, so that
the eunuch saw him no more; and he went on his way
rejoicing. Acts 8:26-39, NKJV

Who was this Ethiopian man? First of all, we know he was a man of great importance and position. At this time in history, Ethiopia was a large and powerful kingdom located south of Egypt, and the treasurer would be similar to our secretary of finance. He would have been a cabinet member, and he would have traveled with a large entourage, including guards.

Picture a stretch chariot with tinted windows. Guys running alongside wearing sunglasses and little radio wires in their ears. He would have been hard to miss.

The Ethiopian diplomat had everything this world can offer. Yet he was on a search for God. We know this because he went to Jerusalem to worship. But instead of finding the vibrant faith of the glory days of Solomon and King David, he found a cold, dead religion that was laden with rules and regulations. Maybe he even tried, as a non-Jew, to keep some of these laws. But there was something missing in his life.

The other man in the story, Philip, did not have earthly power, wealth, or fame. We read early in this chapter that Christians had suddenly turned into public enemy number one. They were being hunted down and killed throughout Judea and Samaria. And yet Philip had the spiritual hope that the Ethiopian was searching for.

All of us are surrounded every day by people just like this Ethiopian man. They're in our churches, our families, our neighborhoods, and our workplaces. They have tried to be religious. Maybe they've prayed, read the Bible, been baptized, gone to church. But something is still missing in their lives, and we have the answer.

MASS VS. ONE-ON-ONE EVANGELISM

Question: Which is better? One-on-one evangelism or stadium evangelism? Why isn't it better to bring a friend to a crusade and let the pros handle things?

Answer: In Acts chapter 8, God gives us a great picture of the upside-down church in action, and we see both kinds of evangelism demonstrated. We see mass, or "crusade," evangelism, which happens in crowds and in group settings. We also see personal evangelism, which happens one-on-one. Both are valid tools.

In the early part of this chapter we read, "Philip went down to the city of Samaria and preached Christ to them. And the multitudes with one accord heeded the things spoken by Philip, hearing and seeing the miracles which he did" (vv. 5-6).

Of THE PEOPLE WHO COME FORWARD AT OUR CRUSADES, AN AVERAGE OF 85 PERCENT ARE BROUGHT BY A FRIEND.

Philip didn't have a stadium, but he might as well have. And this is just one of many examples in Scripture that clearly validate a large-scale approach to evangelization. In part, what kept the crowd attentive to Philip's message were the signs and wonders from God. A similar dynamic is often evident today in our stadium rallies as unbelievers see God in action among thousands of people. Many of these people would never come to church, but what's happening at the stadium captures their attention and makes them more attentive to the gospel message.

As we'll see, most of the principles that apply to personal evangelism also apply to mass evangelism.

The two types often work best in combination. Of the people who come forward at our crusades, an average of 85 percent are brought by a friend.

Keep in mind that both kinds of evangelism—group and individual—are valid and necessary if we're going to change the world.

Our Invisible Needs

Often people don't appear to need a thing, so we pass them by without sharing the gospel. But I'm here to remind you that these are facades. I used to be one of those people. You used to be one of those people, too. And we responded to the gospel.

So before we talk in practical terms about how we witness, let's look at four needs all humans have.

1. PEOPLE ARE SPIRITUALLY EMPTY. Every person has an essential emptiness within that only Christ can fill. In a recent interview Barbara Walters asked highly accomplished actor Richard Dreyfuss a revealing question: "If you could have one wish, what would you wish for?"

Without hesitating, he said, "Every time I have a birthday, every time I blow out candles, every time I see a shooting star, I wish for the same thing—I wish for inner security." Now here is a talented, successful man who still feels something's missing inside.

2. PEOPLE ARE LONELY. We tend to imagine the lonely as shut-ins or widows or people who recently moved to town. We think that the wealthy or famous or important could never be lonely. But everyone who doesn't know Christ is lonely for His companionship. People can only come so close to each other. The great physicist Albert Einstein once wrote to a friend, "It is strange to be known so universally and yet be so lonely." Only Christ can actually come and dwell within us and make His home in us.

3. PEOPLE ARE GUILTY. The Bible tells us that "all have sinned and fall short of the glory of God" (Rom. 3:23, NIV).

Because every person is capable of sin and does sin, every person experiences guilt. Now, not everyone has a strong sense of shame. We can sear our conscience by repeatedly sinning without experiencing repentance. We can also mask our shame with alcohol or suppress feelings of guilt until we convince ourselves that we're essentially good. But deep down every person knows that he or she is out of sync with the Creator.

*E*VERYONE IS EMPTY. EVERYONE IS LONELY. EVERYONE HAS A SENSE OF GUILT. EVERYONE IS AFRAID TO DIE.

4. PEOPLE ARE AFRAID TO DIE. Actor Dennis Hopper was asked about his greatest fear. He gave a one-word answer: "Death." Then he was asked, "What is your greatest regret?" He answered, "Mortality. That you don't live forever."

I know that many unbelievers will strut around and say, "Not me. I'm not afraid to die." But without a sure knowledge of belonging to God, all of us are afraid of death. The only way to truly have peace about our death is to know that heaven awaits us.

We need to allow the Holy Spirit of God to burn these truths into our heart and memory. Everyone is empty. Everyone is lonely. Everyone has a sense of guilt. Everyone is afraid to die. That way, when we look at people, we'll see past the superficial layers to the genuine human needs that make the message of the gospel our only hope.

The Philip Principles

Philip was a little-known disciple, but he became a great evangelist. How did he do it? What were his techniques, and what can we learn from his experiences?

We can learn quite a lot from this ordinary Christian. There are seven vital principles that give us practical guidelines for witnessing. Not only do these principles apply as we evangelize one-on-one, but they also show the way for churches and speakers as they try to reach others for Christ.

1. Go *where people are.*
Remember that Philip had gone to Samaria and preached the gospel. We could read that and not think much of it. But it brings out an important point. The Samaritans and the Jews hated each other. Remember how the woman at the well said to Jesus, "You are a Jew and I am a Samaritan woman. How can you ask me for a drink?" (John 4:9, NIV).

When Philip went to Samaria, he gave up his natural prejudice to bring the gospel to a group of people he would not even have communicated with under normal circumstances.

This reminds us that we should seek to communicate with people who *don't* look just like us. God wants us to take His gospel to *all* people. They may be younger or older or of a different race. There is no room for bigotry, prejudice, or bias in the life of a child of God.

If you want to witness to unbelievers, you need to go to where they live. Maybe it's the beach. Maybe it's the mall. This holds true for mass evangelism or deciding where to start churches. God doesn't tell us to go where people are most likely to come to church and support it financially. God sent Philip to people who needed salvation. It wasn't a great plan for church growth, but it was exactly God's plan for evangelization and soul saving. God did not say that the whole world should go to church but that the church should go to the whole world.

2. Obey *the Spirit's leading.*
Notice these verses from Philip's story: "Now an angel of the Lord spoke to Philip, saying, 'Arise and go toward the south along the road which goes down from Jerusalem to Gaza.' . . .

Then the Spirit said to Philip, 'Go near and overtake this chariot'" (Acts 8:26, 29, NKJV).

You may be thinking, *God never speaks to me.* But consider that the Spirit speaks to you all the time—and maybe you're not listening very well. Some of us tune out things we don't want to hear. We say, "Speak, Lord, your servant is listening." But when He does speak, what we hear doesn't suit us.

SOMETIMES WE DON'T REALIZE THAT WE'VE HEARD GOD UNTIL LATER.

What does God's voice sound like? Thunder? Charlton Heston or George Burns? When God generally speaks to us, it's through our spirit, not through our ears. We have an idea or thought that seems to be from Him. Or we feel what a non-Christian would call a "gut instinct." It may be through a circumstance or even through our own inclinations.

Sometimes we don't realize that we've heard God until later. Did God tell me to talk to the lady at the beach? I believe He did.

But don't miss this: *We don't need to wait to be sure we've heard from God before we evangelize.* He has already spoken to us through His Word. In no uncertain terms He has commanded us to go and preach the gospel. If we see a person bleeding by the side of the road, we don't wait to hear from God about whether or not we should help. We should be taking advantage of every possible opportunity to share our faith. Remember, we scatter our seed wherever we go in the hope that some of it will land on good ground and bring a harvest.

So let's say you've heard the Spirit's leading. Now be sure to obey—no matter how ridiculous the idea may seem. Look at my paraphrase of Philip's story:

> *When Philip hit the streets of Samaria, revival was beginning to break out. Demons were coming out of people. People were being cured of horrible diseases and putting*

their faith in Christ. Then an angel showed up and said,
"Go down toward the desert. That area known as Gaza.
It is about eighty miles from here." Acts 8:5-7, 26

To go eighty miles today, you would hop in your car and be there in just over an hour. But for Philip it meant a very long, hot walk. How easily Philip could have said, "Excuse me, Lord, but with all due respect, the apostles and the other believers in Jerusalem are at least thirty miles closer. Couldn't you call one of them? Great things are happening right here."

But Philip responded and seized the moment. And it's a good thing, because God had uniquely equipped him to deal with this man from Ethiopia. And God has uniquely equipped each of us as well if we'll obey His leading.

3. Approach with tact.
So you've decided to approach some middle-aged lady on the beach with God's good news. Where should you start? Probably not with, "Hey, sinner!"

Philip used tact. I love the way he approached this Ethiopian in the chariot. He didn't walk up to him and say, "Excuse me, are you saved?" or "Did you know you are going to hell?"

Instead, he sought to establish a dialogue. "Excuse me, do you understand what you are reading?"

I wonder if that Ethiopian thought, *And you are? . . . Do you normally hang out by yourself in the middle of the desert?*

Tact has been defined as the intuitive knowledge of saying the right thing at the right time. And I hate to say it, but this skill is sorely lacking in many Christians. When the Bible says preach, it doesn't necessarily mean you have to yell or be rude. Some perfectly friendly people turn into "droids" or tape recordings when they start to talk about Jesus.

But we can preach the gospel conversationally. We're not speaking from the steps of the Lincoln Memorial. We can stumble a bit, ask questions, look the person in the eye. We can remind ourselves that we're talking to someone who is just like us.

IN CONVERSATION, UNEXPECTED DOORS OF OPPORTUNITY CAN OPEN AS WE LEARN MORE ABOUT A PERSON.

Which brings up a possible language barrier: I call it "Christianese." Say you approach an unbeliever and begin, "Hey, you reprobate! Has anyone ever told you that you are lost, perishing, damned, and headed for perdition? What you need to do is be regenerated. Converted through repentance. And then you need to get on the straight and narrow!"

Now what exactly does that mean? For an unbeliever it means don't maintain eye contact and leave as soon as possible. If we use biblical terms—and some of them, like *salvation, redemption,* and *justification* are indispensable—we need to define our terms as we go. Effective evangelists always explain key concepts in familiar terms.

4. Establish common ground.

Philip took time to assess the Ethiopian's situation and relate to him as a person, not just as a potential convert. Here was this guy, reading from Isaiah 53. So Philip offered his help, conversed with him, and got to know him a little bit.

Sometimes it's only as we talk to people about life in general that we perceive the best way to bring the gospel to them. In conversation, unexpected doors of opportunity can open as we learn more about a person. And if we first affirm the other's feelings—"I understand. . . . I used to think that. . . ."—then the person is more open to our explanation of what we know to be true.

This also means that we adapt to people. It doesn't mean we change or adapt the gospel; we simply acknowledge that although everyone is essentially the same—empty, lonely, guilty, and afraid to die—we are at different stages in life and are facing our own unique joys and challenges. If we're going to share the gospel message with someone, we need to be willing to put ourself in that person's shoes for a moment and to express ourself so that we can be understood.

Paul put it this way in 1 Corinthians 9:19-23:

> *This means I am not bound to obey people just because they pay me, yet I have become a servant of everyone so that I can bring them to Christ. When I am with the Jews, I become one of them so that I can bring them to Christ. When I am with those who follow the Jewish laws, I do the same, even though I am not subject to the law, so that I can bring them to Christ. When I am with the Gentiles who do not have the Jewish law, I fit in with them as much as I can. In this way, I gain their confidence and bring them to Christ. But I do not discard the law of God; I obey the law of Christ. When I am with those who are oppressed, I share their oppression so that I might bring them to Christ. Yes, I try to find common ground with everyone so that I might bring them to Christ. I do all this to spread the Good News, and in doing so I enjoy its blessings.* NLT

Jesus, the master communicator, never dealt with any two people in exactly the same way. The woman at the well had spent a lifetime trying to fill a void with men. Jesus spoke of her deep spiritual thirst. To an expert in theology, Jesus spoke in almost childlike terms as He told Nicodemus in John 3 that he must be born again.

Keep this point in mind whenever you are talking to someone about the gospel. Establish relationship, and then, based on what you learn, ask yourself, *What gospel story or image would this person connect with?*

That leads us to our next point: We need to know the Bible.

5. *Use God's Word.*
"Then Philip opened his mouth, and beginning at this Scripture, preached Jesus to him."

This, of course, is an essential for any person who wants to lead others to Jesus Christ. We are told in 2 Timothy 2:15 (paraphrased), "Study or exert yourself to be approved by God, a workman that does not need to be ashamed, rightly dividing the Word of truth."

Why is it important to share Scripture? Because the Word of God will not return void. I have found that when I am sharing the gospel, whether through preaching or one-on-one, the most powerful tool I have is the Word of God. Greg's word returns void. God's Word does not.

God says in Isaiah 55:10-11:

> As the rain comes down, and the snow from heaven, and do not return there, but water the earth, and make it bring forth and bud, that it may give seed to the sower and bread to the eater, so shall My word be that goes forth from My mouth; it shall not return to Me void, but it shall accomplish what I please, and it shall prosper in the thing for which I sent it. NKJV

Billy Graham once said, "Time and time again in my ministry I have quoted a Bible verse in a sermon, sometimes without planning to do so in advance, only to have someone tell me afterwards it was that verse that the Holy Spirit used to bring conviction and faith to him."

What if Philip had not been a student of the Bible when he was asked, "Of whom is the prophet speaking? Of himself or another?" If Philip hadn't been a student of Scripture, he would have said, "I don't know. A good question. Can I get back to you?" But fortunately Philip was well versed in what the Bible taught.

This doesn't mean you shouldn't witness because you don't have a lot of Scripture memorized or that the person who knows the most Scripture is the most effective witness. I'm saying that this is a powerful tool, an important tool, and you should always be trying to grow in your knowledge of the Word. We need to study and prepare ourselves as effectively as possible.

First Peter 3:15 says, "In your hearts set apart Christ as Lord. Always be prepared to give an answer to everyone who asks you to give the reason for the hope that you have. But do this with gentleness and respect" (NIV).

Notice that it's not just the Word quoted but an appropriate passage that relates to the person or situation you are addressing. Scripture reminds us, "A word fitly spoken is like apples of gold in settings of silver" (Prov. 25:11, NKJV).

> *THE BIBLE IS THE WORD OF GOD WHETHER PEOPLE ACCEPT IT OR NOT.*

And if you don't have the answer? That's OK. Simply let that propel you back into the pages of Scripture to find it.

Some people might say to you, "I don't believe the Bible is the Word of God. That is *your* truth. Don't push your truth on me." They can say whatever they want. The Bible is the Word of God whether they accept it or not. And it is going to touch their life.

They may get angry. They might be resistant. But Scripture has a way of penetrating. Use it, know it, learn it, and memorize it.

6. Tell your story.
When you present the gospel, one of the most effective tools is the story of how you yourself came to Christ. It's a great way to share the gospel with people without making them feel preached at. And it is also a great way to offer proof that an intimate relationship with God is possible.

The book of Acts is full of examples where those preaching used their personal testimony. So often Paul would tell his own story, explaining how he used to persecute Christians and how he met the Lord on the way to Damascus. Keep in mind that Paul had a great intellect. He not only had a tremendous grasp of Scripture, but he was schooled in Roman culture and debate. Yet in so many cases when appearing before the elite of Rome, he would begin with that simple story of how he personally came to Christ.

A GOOD TESTIMONY IS ONE THAT DOES NOT GLORIFY THE PAST BUT GLORIFIES WHAT GOD IS DOING IN YOUR LIFE IN THE PRESENT.

Let me throw in a caution here, however. A good testimony is one that does not glorify the past. It glorifies what God is doing in your life in the present. I have heard people get up and talk about their life before the Lord and all the horrible things they used to do. And as they were describing it, it almost seemed that they had more fun before they became a Christian.

You also want to avoid focusing on what you have given up. "I had the success and the fame and fortune. But I gave it all up for Jesus!" When you say something like that, you are putting the emphasis on the wrong thing. You ought to be emphasizing what

Christ gave up for you. Prior to knowing Christ, you were an empty, guilty person headed for certain judgment. All you gave up was an eternity separated from God. That was no sacrifice.

7. Pursue a decision.

Philip read the account of the death of Jesus to the Ethiopian. He pointed out that it was Jesus whom Isaiah was speaking of. Jesus was the Son of God, who went to the cross. Jesus was the one who shed His blood for us and died and rose from the dead. Jesus is the one we need.

The man said, "I want it." He invited the Lord into his life. And we're told that he "went away rejoicing."

It's tempting to just chitchat and call it good. "Wow. We had a great conversation about all kinds of spiritual issues." That's OK. But Jesus cut to the chase: "But who do you say that I am?" (Matt. 16:15, NKJV). There may be situations in which we are employing a long-term strategy, say, with a family member or coworker. But whenever possible after we share the gospel, we should ask the person to respond. The worst thing that could happen is that we get killed for asking. Since that is highly unlikely, consider two other alternatives.

The person might simply say no. That is a disappointment, but that may change tomorrow, so there's still hope.

But what about this alternative: A person might say yes and commit his or her life to Christ. If so, you will have had the privilege of personally leading someone from darkness to light.

Look Up

You might say, "God never gives me these opportunities."

But I suggest to you that He does. They are there. As Jesus pointed out, "The harvest is plentiful, lift up your eyes." The harvest is there, but the laborers are few. The observers are many. The critics are many. The complainers and "pew potatoes" are many. But the laborers are few.

Start where you are. Reach your world. Reach the people who are around you. You can reach them more effectively than many others can.

"But I'm not a professional!"

I'm so glad of that.

May God deliver us from many of these so-called professionals, who often do more harm than good. We need to do what we can to reach with the gospel the people God has already put under our influence. If you're not a professional, that's probably more an asset than it is a liability. You're just a regular person, nonintimidating, who speaks their language.

It's easy to spend a lot of time preparing to witness, working up our courage, thinking through our approach—only to discover that we're still pretty vague about the message we're delivering. We're still a bit mystified about what happened in that brief space in Scripture between when Philip met the Ethiopian and the Ethiopian believed, because it doesn't always go that smoothly.

We need to know exactly what the gospel message is and how best to explain it.

SIX

THE GOSPEL ACCORDING TO GOD

There's Good News—and Some Bad News

I HEARD a story once about a group of servicemen who had a new chaplain appointed to them. These guys weren't believers, and they wondered what kind of religion this fellow really had. They approached the new chaplain and said, "Tell us, do you believe in a real hell?"

"A literal hell?" the chaplain asked.

"Yes, that's the one," one of them answered.

The chaplain, who was rather liberal in his theology, said, "No, rest assured, boys, I don't believe in a literal hell."

He thought this would make them happy. But their response surprised him. They said, "Well then, you are wasting your time and our time, because if there is no hell, we don't need you. But if there is a hell, you're leading us astray. Either way we're better off without you."

Sometimes I wonder if we Christians honestly believe what we claim to believe. Do we *really* believe the wages of sin is death? Do we *really* believe in heaven and hell? If that's the case—if we believe there really is hell—why are we not doing more to reach people with the gospel of Jesus Christ?

In the previous two chapters we looked at two reasons we don't evangelize. We're uncaring, and we're uncomfortable.

Now we're going to look at a third possible problem: We're unconvinced. Do we really know the gospel message? And do we really believe it?

Many years ago in England a criminal named Charles Peace was arrested. He was a burglar and a forger, and he was guilty of double murder. He was condemned to death. As he was on his way to the gallows to be executed, the chaplain who walked by his side went mechanically through his speech about the power of Jesus Christ to save from sin. Suddenly this criminal stopped, spun around, and looked at the minister and said, "Do you believe that? Do you really believe that? If I believed that, I would willingly crawl across England on broken glass to tell men it was true."

Today's church finds itself unable to turn the world upside down because in many ways it has compromised the very message that would accomplish this.

I believe the church today finds itself unable to turn the world upside down because in many ways it has compromised the very message that would accomplish this. Instead of proclaiming the gospel according to God, we are so often tempted to preach the gospel according to what we or our hearers might like. We can't evangelize if we're unconvinced—or if we don't really believe the whole gospel.

I read in a recent survey that 75 percent of the American public do not know what John 3:16 says. And 60-some percent don't know what the word *gospel* actually means.

Certainly *gospel* is tossed around loosely today. We describe a certain kind of music as gospel music. Or if we are stating something that we want people to know is true, we might say, "That's the gospel truth, I'm telling you!"

Or we will hear someone preaching and that person will say, "I am an evangelist. I am preaching the gospel." But then as we listen carefully, we realize that we are not hearing the gospel of Jesus Christ.

We need to know what the gospel is. What elements does the true gospel contain? This is important for two reasons. First, we want to make sure we've heard the true message and have responded to it, lest we build our faith on a false foundation. And second, Jesus has commanded every one of us to go into the world and preach this message—so we'd better know exactly what it is.

The Heart of His Message

The heart of the great commission is God's amazing upside-down message of salvation. A good summation is given to us by Paul in 1 Corinthians 15:2-4: "By this gospel you are saved. . . . Christ died for our sins according to the Scriptures . . . he was buried . . . he was raised on the third day according to the Scriptures" (NIV).

This is the gospel in a nutshell: Christ died for our sins, was buried, and was raised on the third day. But what exactly does this mean to the new believer? And why does it mean so much?

It's easy for us who have been Christians a long time to forget the basic principles of this incredible life-changing event we call salvation. We may think we know this message well, but as we seek to articulate its principles to an unbeliever, we often find ourselves stumbling.

WE MAY THINK WE KNOW THIS MESSAGE WELL, BUT AS WE SEEK TO ARTICULATE ITS PRINCIPLES TO AN UNBELIEVER, WE OFTEN FIND OURSELVES STUMBLING.

As we take a closer look at the meaning of salvation, we see that through salvation, we are acquitted of sin, allotted Christ's righteousness, and adopted into God's family. Those sound like a lot of lofty words, and for that reason alone we need to look at what they mean so that we can explain salvation clearly and simply to unbelievers.

1. We are acquitted of sin.
The apostle Paul put it this way in his letter to the Romans:

> *Therefore, having been justified by faith, we have peace with God through our Lord Jesus Christ, through whom also we have access by faith into this grace in which we stand, and rejoice in hope of the glory of God.*
> Rom. 5:1-2, NKJV

There's a phrase here I don't want you to miss: "justified by faith."

Justification sounds like a complicated word, but the idea is simple. It describes a legal act of God whereby you are declared guiltless before Him and are acquitted of every sin. Not because you are worthy or innocent—but because Christ stepped up and took your place.

It's as if Christ announced, "Hey, I did it. I'm guilty. Kill me instead." And because you agreed to let Him take your place, you were acquitted. Paul put it this way: "Christ redeemed us from the curse of the law by becoming a curse for us" (Gal. 3:13, NIV).

And to the Romans he wrote, "[We] are justified freely by his grace through the redemption that came by Christ Jesus. God presented him as a sacrifice of atonement, through faith in his blood" (Rom. 3:24-25, NIV).

Now if justification simply stated that my past was forgiven, that would be more than enough. But as they say in those commercials, "Wait, there's more!"

2. We are allotted Christ's righteousness.

Justification not only speaks of the sin God has taken away but of what He has allotted to us in its place. The word *justified* can be translated "put to one's account." When God justifies people, He places to their credit all the righteousness of Jesus Christ. And in doing so, He balances the moral and spiritual budget for us.

Philippians 3:9 says, "Not having my own righteousness, which is from the law, but that which is through faith in Christ, the righteousness which is from God by faith" (NKJV). This is not something that happens over a period of time, if you earn it. It is something that is instantaneously allotted to every person who has put his or her faith in Christ. No matter what they have done. It is not gradual; it is immediate.

Here's one way to think about it. Imagine that you were in debt for $10 million. You had charged yourself into oblivion, and there was no conceivable way you could pay back those debts. You had exactly $1.34 in your checking account.

Now imagine that a stranger came to you and said, "I love you so much that I am going to pay off your debts." And he paid off your debt of $10 million.

"Thank you so much!" you'd exclaim. "I can't believe I'm debt free!"

Then the stranger says, "I think you ought to go down and check your account balance."

So you go down to your local ATM machine and put in your card and code. The machine prints the little report. You have a balance of $20 million! Not only did he forgive you a debt of $10 million and pay it for you—he put into your account $20 million. Think about that. What God did for you is infinitely greater than that. God not only acquitted you of your sins, but He also allotted to your account the righteousness of Jesus Christ.

But wait. There's still more!

3. We are adopted into God's family.

Not only has God forgiven you, not only has God justified you, not only has God given you free access into His presence, but God has also adopted you into His family. The Bible tells us in Galatians 4:4-5: "When the fullness of the time had come, God sent forth His son, born of a woman, born under the law, to redeem those who were under the law, that we might receive the adoption as sons" (NKJV).

I can stand in awe of a God who has the power to forgive me and the desire to put His righteousness into my account. But by adopting me God is saying, "Don't just stand there in awe of me. Come close to me."

Justification speaks of an incredible thing done on my behalf. But adoption speaks of relationship. God says, "I want you as my son. I want you as my daughter."

Years ago, when I was in Israel, I saw a little Israeli boy chasing after his father, crying out, "Abba, Abba, Abba." I knew what that meant. It would be the same as if we saw a child chasing after his or her father saying, "Daddy, Daddy, Daddy." *Abba* is a Hebrew word that speaks of affection and intimacy between a parent and a child.

Galatians 4:6 continues: "Because you are sons, God has sent forth the Spirit of His Son into your hearts, crying out, 'Abba, Father!'" And then in Romans 8:15: "You did not receive the spirit of bondage again to fear, but you received the Spirit of adoption by whom we cry out, 'Abba, Father.'" Remember, this was a revolutionary thought to the people at that time. One didn't think of approaching the almighty, all-powerful, holy God and saying, "Abba." But Jesus was saying, "Yes, I have justified you. Yes, I have forgiven you. And what's more, I want you to come close.

This is the message we need to make known to a lost and dying culture. Remember, the gospel is the same for every person. We may relate it to different people in different ways. But the basics, the essentials, never change."

The gospel is capable of reaching every person. It cuts through cultural barriers, racial barriers, economic barriers, and age barriers. Everybody can grasp it because God honors and blesses it and somehow drives it into the heart of the listener.

Whether we're evangelizing one-on-one or in a church setting, we don't need to candy coat the gospel. We don't need to gloss over it. We don't need to soften it or harden it. We don't need to take away from it or add to it. We need to proclaim it in its simplicity and power and stand back and watch what God can do.

> *THE GOSPEL CUTS THROUGH CULTURAL, RACIAL, ECONOMIC, AND AGE BARRIERS.*

Paul said, "I am not ashamed of the gospel of Christ, for it is the power of God to salvation for everyone who believes" (Rom. 1:16, NKJV).

Remember, Paul was a great orator. He was a student and a communicator. Paul could have called upon his ability to convince. He could have called upon his powers of oratory to bring his listeners around. But instead Paul concentrated on that simple-yet-profound gospel message because he recognized that it, not he, is the power of God that brings people into God's kingdom.

When we give invitations for people to come to Christ here in our church and at our crusades, we believe it is a work of God. My goal is not to get as many people on the field as possible. My goal is to proclaim the gospel as accurately as I can and leave the work of conversion up to the Holy Spirit.

EVANGELISM OR ENTERTAINMENT?

Question: How does Harvest Christian Fellowship decide what kinds of entertainment, drama, music, and recreation are an appropriate part of spreading the gospel, and what kinds aren't? Any criteria?

Answer: I look for a clear and uncompromised message. Otherwise, why would the church want to sponsor it? I also look for high quality.

If we are going to have a musical artist, I want to have personally seen the artist in action or have an endorsement from someone I can trust. Merely listening to the CD or reading the press packet is not really very helpful in making the evaluation.

I want musicians, actors, and worship leaders who are talented and relevant, but what is most important is that they use their gifts to minister to people rather than to put on a show. We like to embrace many musical styles at Harvest. Our criteria are authenticity, compassion, and a heart for God's kingdom and people.

PASTOR TO PASTOR
"Come On Down!"

Some time ago I saw a preacher on TV giving an invitation for people to come to Christ. The choir was singing "Just As I Am." (This was not Billy Graham, by the way). The pastor said, "If you want to come to Christ, get up and come forward now."

The camera went in for a long shot, and you could see the whole congregation. A couple of people trickled down front. Obviously the pastor was not happy with the number of people who were responding. So he said, "If you would like to make a recommitment to follow Jesus Christ, then you get up and come down." A couple of other people got up. But it was still pretty empty up there. And then the pastor actually said, "If you would like to know more about joining the church, come down now."

When he got to "If you want to join the choir, come down," I thought to myself, *Why doesn't he just say, "If you want to examine the veneer of the wood on my pulpit, come on down. Just don't leave me up here alone!"*

Sometimes we pastors get to thinking that our objective is to make people respond to God. But that's not your job or my job. Our job is to make the message clear and leave the results up to God. If people believe, that is the work of the Holy Spirit.

The Gospel Unplugged

We've looked at how to overcome some of our practical inhibitions about witnessing to other people. In fact, we followed Philip through a lot of key steps, right up to the point of baptizing the Ethiopian.

But now I want to talk to you about the presentation of the gospel. It doesn't always go as smoothly as it did for me that day at the beach or as it did for Philip and the Ethiopian. As we all know, it's one thing to understand the gospel message and quite another to present it, especially when our audience is skeptical or argumentative. We tend to get sidetracked, and sometimes we lose the basic message.

SOMETIMES WE PASTORS GET TO THINKING THAT OUR JOB IS TO MAKE PEOPLE RESPOND TO GOD.

Think about music. There are a million ways to dress it up—add electric guitars, keyboards, strings. Have you ever known a song really well and then one day you heard a version of it that was "unplugged"? Probably the beauty and simplicity of it was stunning. Suddenly you heard the simple melody and message of that song.

It's the same with the gospel. Presentation matters. We have a lot of high-tech approaches, especially in churches that are aiming at consumers instead of communers. The same tactics that work for other kinds of messages—such as business ads or political campaigns—backfire when it comes to the gospel.

From the world's viewpoint, God's kingdom operates upside down. So why would we imagine we should sell it as if it were any popular club or zippy new philosophy? Why do we think it's necessary to disguise its key points? I think we often underestimate the raw, even explosive, power that is inherent in the "unplugged" gospel message.

The same tactics that work for other kinds of messages—such as business ads or political campaigns—backfire when it comes to the gospel.

The gospel according to God is simple. It is uncompromising, powerful, and complete. If you want to present Christ's message so that people become Christians in your church, or outside your church, keep the following principles in mind.

1. The gospel doesn't need our help.

I am amazed time and time again when people say, "Greg, what are you going to preach on this year at the crusade?"

"Same thing I preached last year. I am going to preach the gospel."

"What is your text?"

"The text may be different. The illustrations may be different. But it is going to be the same message."

"Yeah, but what about the Generation Xers? How are you going to communicate with them?"

Well, God doesn't change the basic truths according to who's attending the crusade. And God's Holy Spirit can convince anyone—Gen Xers included—that they need to be saved from their sins. If we tell the truth, God will use it.

2. *The most effective message is a simple one.*
Someone once asked the great British preacher C. H. Spurgeon if he could put in a few words what his Christian faith was all about. Spurgeon said, "I will put it into four words for you. Christ died for me."

It's as simple as that. Christ died for me. That is the essence of the gospel message. I love the way the apostle Paul said that God "loved me and gave himself for me" (Gal. 2:20, NIV).

Some time ago I had the privilege of watching Billy Graham receive the Congressional Medal of Honor in our nation's Capitol building for his faithfulness in preaching the gospel. The ceremony took place in the rotunda, a very imposing and intimidating room with a giant ceiling and incredible paintings and statues of presidents and other figures of American history.

Many members of Congress, as well as the vice president, were present. On a raised platform in the back of the rotunda, cameras from around the world filmed the event. Now if ever there would have been a temptation to soften the gospel a bit, to simply say a few nice things, that would have been it.

But one of the things I love about Billy Graham is that he is so tenacious. And he knows what he is supposed to do. He got up there and opened with a few pleasantries. And then he began to preach the gospel. He said, "I want to tell you that many years ago I was a young boy, and I went to a meeting. A man was telling us that we were sinners and we needed Christ. And he said,  'All have sinned and fallen short of the glory of God.' And right then, I realized I needed Christ to come into my life."

After presenting the gospel in simple, beautiful terms, he brought it all home. "As I look around at these statues of all of

These great leaders ... have one thing in common. They are all dead. And you are all going to die.

these great leaders, I realize that they have one thing in common. They are all dead. And you are all going to die. Are you ready to die? Are you ready to meet God?"

I loved that. Remember, fellow communicators, that you and I can actually hinder the message of the gospel by complicating it. The same thing goes for you, layperson, when you're talking one-on-one with an unbeliever in some coffee shop. And so we need to be careful to present the simple, powerful, yet profound truth. Christ died for our sins. He was buried. He was raised again on the third day. Are you ready to die?

3. The good news of the gospel includes some bad news.
The word *gospel* actually means "good news." But before I can appreciate the good news of forgiveness, I need to know the bad news about judgment. If we don't deliver the whole truth of the gospel, we are not proclaiming the gospel.

You and I can actually hinder the message of the gospel by complicating it.

This is where I take issue with people who offer Jesus as though He were some kind of a wonderful additive to life. "Accept Jesus Christ, and your teeth will be whiter, and your clothes will be cleaner, and your life will be better. Everything will be great."

But Christianity is not just about being happier. It's not about being a little bit more fulfilled. *It's about not going to hell,* and if you reject God's offer of salvation—you will face certain judgment.

The other day I was with my wife in a department store. She was looking at dresses, and I was wandering around. A salesgirl came up to me and said, "Are you Greg Laurie?"

"Yes, I am."

She said, "I can't believe you're here. My girlfriend and I were just talking about you. Actually, we were just talking with a

friend who works in another department. He is living an immoral lifestyle. He was saying it's OK to be a Christian and live
that way. If you could just talk to him, we think he would really
listen to you."

I said, "OK. But tell him what he is getting himself into. Tell
him that I'm a pastor and that I am going to tell him what the
Bible says. I don't want him to think
that he's being trapped."

So she and her friend went and
got this guy and introduced us. "By
the way, he's a homosexual," they
announced.

This guy was obviously not happy
about talking to me, and for a few
moments we both just stood there,
feeling somewhat awkward. "I don't really think it's appropriate
to talk about this here," he finally said. "But let me just say this
really quick. I believe in Jesus Christ. But my God is a god of love,
and I don't believe He'd send someone to hell for doing what I am
doing. I believe that if two consenting adults agree to do something, it can't be wrong. How can you say that's sin?"

My response to him was, "Because God says it's sin."

I know that sounds simplistic, but that really is the bottom
line. "You say that you believe in a God of love," I said. "I believe in a God of love, too. But when you say 'my God,' you are
implying that you can remake Him in your image. You can't
throw out the things about God that bother you and keep the
ones you like. Who determines what is right and what is wrong?
Do we reach it by consensus? No. We need a higher authority.
And it's the Bible."

We talked for quite a while about what the Bible says. Finally
he said, "I don't believe that God would say I can't do this one
thing. I am going to keep doing it. I don't care what happens."

I knew I had to tell this guy the truth, so I said, "Well, I have to

WE MISTAKENLY OFFER GOD'S FORGIVENESS WITHOUT ANY MENTION OF REPENTANCE.

put it to you bluntly. If you continue living that way, you will face judgment for it." I spoke to him of God's plan and purpose. He didn't make a decision for Christ, but he said he was going to come to church.

So often we're tempted to offer a watered-down gospel with no teeth in it. We offer God's forgiveness without any mention of repentance. I've heard people use phrases like "All you have to do is ask Him in. That's it. It's wonderful."

WE HAVE TO TAKE TIME TO LOOK AT THE BAD NEWS—SIN AND JUDGMENT—BEFORE THE GOOD NEWS HAS MEANING.

Wait a second. What about repentance? What about obedience?

We have to take time to look at the bad news—sin and sure judgment—before the Good News has meaning. We have to acknowledge the exceeding sinfulness of humanity. We are hopelessly separated from a holy God whom we have all offended. There is nothing good in ourselves, and we desperately need His help.

And then comes the good news. In spite of our condition, regardless of all of the wrong things we've done, God did the ultimate for us. Romans 5:6 says:

When we were still without strength, in due time Christ died for the ungodly. For scarcely for a righteous man will one die; yet perhaps for a good man someone would even dare to die. But God demonstrates His own love toward us, in that while we were still sinners, Christ died for us. NKJV

4. A compromising gospel is no gospel.
In 1 Timothy 4:16 Paul says, "Watch your life and doctrine closely. Persevere in them, because if you do, you will save both yourself and your hearers" (NIV). We must know what we believe.

We must know what the Bible teaches, especially on the topic of the gospel. Why? Because there is a counterfeit gospel out there.

Make no mistake about it. The devil is a master manipulator and imitator. One of the greatest tactics that he has used with tremendous effect over the centuries is to imitate "good news"—to offer a counterfeit version of it that is close enough to be believable to some but far enough from truth to be damaging to the person who believes it.

Paul wrote in Galatians 1:6-8:

> *I am astonished that you are so quickly deserting the one who called you by the grace of Christ and are turning to a different gospel—which is really no gospel at all. Evidently some people are throwing you into confusion and are trying to pervert the gospel of Christ. But even if we or an angel from heaven should preach a gospel other than the one we preached to you, let him be eternally condemned!* NIV

One consistent criticism of Christianity is, "How can you say as a Christian that Christ is the only way to God? Are you saying that people who have other religious beliefs are not believing the true thing? Are you saying that your way is the only way? How narrow of you. How bigoted of you."

It can be tempting to soft-pedal this issue and say something along the lines of "We all worship the same God. And you can choose your path. I have chosen mine. Mine is Christ. But if you want to worship some other way, that is fine."

None of the other gurus and prophets and religious leaders that have come down the road were God.

It's not fine. And you can't say it if you are a true Christian. We must believe that Jesus is the only way to God, because none of the other gurus and prophets and religious leaders that have come down the road *were* God. Therefore, none of them could put us in touch with God. Even if they had been crucified as Jesus was, it would not have mattered. Jesus, who was God, was the only one who could bridge the gap and shed His blood in our place.

Jesus himself is the one who said this. He said in John 14:6, "I am the way and the truth and the life. No one comes to the Father except through me" (NIV). The apostle Peter echoed these words when he said in Acts 4:12, "Salvation is found in no one else, for there is no other name under heaven given to men by which we must be saved" (NIV). Paul says the same thing in 1 Timothy 2:5: "There is one God and one mediator between God and men, the man Christ Jesus" (NIV).

Therefore, to properly represent Jesus' message I can say nothing less.

Some of you may be thinking, *But if I say that to people, they will be offended.*

Maybe they will be. Then again, maybe they will believe. Who am I to edit the gospel? Who am I to say, "Lord, we need to update this whole thing for this new century. The words you spoke were insensitive and politically incorrect. We don't talk about hell anymore. We don't talk about sin anymore. This stuff is out, Lord."

We need to give His message and not change it—not even a little bit. Because there's nothing more exciting than the message of the gospel. And when we embrace it in its simplest, truest form and determine to preach it in a radical, upside-down way, we are in for the greatest thrill of our life.

PASTOR TO PASTOR
The Gift of Evangelism

Now and then I have a pastor say to me, "I'm just not very gifted at evangelism." If this is your case, I suggest that you find someone in your body who does

have the calling and gifts of an evangelist and give him
a platform for ministry.

All of us are not "gifted in evangelism," but *all of us*
are called to evangelize and to support evangelism in its
various forms. Paul wrote to Timothy, an overseer of a
church, and told him to "do the work of an evangelist"
(2 Tim. 4:5, NIV).

We often think that the work of the evangelist is done
only outside the church. But that is not true. In Ephesians
4:11-12 we read, "And He Himself gave some to be
apostles, some prophets, some evangelists, and some
pastors and teachers, for the equipping of the saints"
(NKJV). A person gifted for evangelism will not only bring
the gospel message to the lost but will often have a special
exhortive ability (to motivate, stimulate, excite to action)
for the church. This is a simplification, but in one sense
a pastor tells you how to do it while an evangelist makes
you want to do it!

SEVEN

WALK THIS WAY
The Meaning of Upside-Down Discipleship

DON'T YOU love it when you're reading along in the Old Testament and suddenly God slows everything down to tell an important story? Time and again we pause in the history of God's people to zoom in on an unlikely hero, a conflict that threatens, and a detailed account of how things were finally resolved God's way.

The account in Judges of Gideon's battling the Midianites is one of these amazing stories. At the time, the Israelites were being plagued by their enemies, the Midianites, and an alliance of other hostile nations. God's answer was to choose a regular guy named Gideon to lead an army against them. The story begins in Judges 6.

Just how ordinary was Gideon? Well, the angel sent as a messenger from God caught Gideon in the act of being a coward. Gideon was so afraid of being seen by the enemy that he was secretly threshing his wheat inside a winepress—not on the community threshing floor—so no one would see him. But the angel greeted him with a memorable one-liner: "The Lord is with you, mighty warrior!"

We can almost hear Gideon laugh (or maybe it's the angel).

Gideon answers the angel as many of us would. "Hey, if God

is with me, then why are all these bad things happening? We're all at the end of our rope here. And in case you didn't notice, my family happens to be the weakest one around, and what's more, I'm the least among them! You must be looking for someone else!" (see Judg. 6:13-15).

Isn't it interesting how we always feel certain that God has the wrong man or woman whenever He's recruiting us? But the whole time, God is thinking, *You're just what I had in mind.*

In Judges 6:14 the angel of the Lord turned to Gideon and said something very important. "Go in the strength you have and save Israel out of Midian's hand. Am I not sending you?" (NIV).

Remember that line: "Go in the strength you have. Am I not sending you?"

So Gideon raised up an army of men to war against their enemies. But even with a thirty-two-thousand-man force the Israelite army was still far outnumbered by the Midianite alliance. Naturally Gideon wondered how and where on earth he'd find more men.

But here's what God said to Gideon. "You have too many men for me to deliver Midian into their hands" (Judg. 7:2, NIV).

Obviously Gideon was coming face-to-face with a God whose ways are upside down in relation to ours. And as Gideon tried not to choke on his breakfast, God set about reducing the size of Israel's army. First, He told Gideon to ask those soldiers to leave who were afraid. So Gideon did. Twenty-two thousand said, "Sure thing. I wasn't in the mood to die, anyway." And they left.

Gideon must have thought: *God sure underestimated how many were afraid!*

Not at all. In fact, God said to Gideon, "Still too many men are left." Then He told Gideon to take the remaining ten thousand men down to the river to drink. God instructed Gideon to let the very thirsty men drink their fill. He was to then watch for the ones who brought the water to their mouth cupped in their hand. Presumably they would be the watchful, alert, prepared ones, aware of a potential enemy ambush.

Gideon now had a mighty army of a few hundred men. Only those who were bravest and who were wholeheartedly committed to the battle were left. Finally God was ready to go to work. In a daring night raid, God gave Gideon's army a stunning victory over the Midianites. You can read more about how God went about doing this in Judges 7.

GOD CAN DO MORE WITH A FEW COMMITTED FOLKS THAN HE CAN WITH THOUSANDS WHO ARE FOLLOWING HIM ONLY HALFHEARTEDLY.

Through stories like Gideon's, God makes it abundantly and repeatedly clear that He can do more with a few committed folks than He can with thousands who are following Him only halfheartedly. Today God is still looking around to see who He really has. He is seeking those men and women who will follow Him with total abandon—against all odds, without questioning His directions or His methods.

God is looking for true disciples who are willing to think and act according to God's upside-down terms. God is looking for churches and pastors who are ready—no matter how small their congregations or poor their people or old their buildings—to turn their cities upside down for Christ.

"Am I not sending you?" He asks. "So go in the strength you have."

Hard Words

In many ways the first church found itself in a position similar to Gideon's. They were completely outnumbered, and their task appeared ridiculous, even impossible. To spread the gospel to every nation? To make the whole world believe in this Jesus who came and died and was resurrected? To get the world to follow a man they couldn't see?

In the last few chapters we saw how the early believers succeeded in their mission. But why were they able to do this? Not because they were mighty or numerous, or because they were brilliant strategic thinkers and marketers. But because they were true disciples who were taking directions from God.

Let's look first at the statements of Jesus concerning what is required in order for us to become His disciples. But let me make this doubly clear: These statements are *not* Jesus' requirements for salvation. When we first come to Jesus Christ to receive the salvation He has offered us, we are at the beginning of a lifelong process. We are new to faith; maybe it's the first time in our life we've accepted anybody's authority. But as we grow in our faith and truly follow Christ, we're able to understand the realities of spiritual battle and of how radical our lifestyle is in an unbelieving world. Becoming a Christian requires a change of heart and a choice; continuing on in discipleship, becoming part of God's spiritual army on earth, has its own requirements.

Jesus decided to say some very hard things to these adoring masses and to all who would one day follow Him, including you and me.

First, let me set the scene. A great crowd had begun to follow Jesus at this point in His ministry. He'd become very popular with the common people because they resonated deeply with His message. They appreciated Jesus for deflating the religious establishment, for revealing the Pharisees to be the hypocrites they were, and for preaching about a kingdom that was available to everyone.

So here were all these people listening raptly to Jesus. These were Jesus' fans, and they loved Him. When things are going this well, most of us would be inclined to give the crowd what they want. Make them glad to be here. Make them want to stay—and, more important, get them on our computerized mailing list!

But Jesus did something very upside down. Just when you would think Jesus would be wanting to gather an army of followers, He made a Gideon move. He decided to say some very hard things to these adoring masses and to all who would one day follow Him, including you and me. Three times in the verses that we're about to read He says, "cannot be my disciple." He is saying, "You must do these things or you can't be my disciple."

Now great multitudes went with Him. And He turned and said to them, "If anyone comes to Me and does not hate his father and mother, wife and children, brothers and sisters, yes, and his own life also, he cannot be My disciple. And whoever does not bear his cross and come after Me cannot be My disciple. For which of you, intending to build a tower, does not sit down first and count the cost, whether he has enough to finish it—lest, after he has laid the foundation, and is not able to finish, all who see it begin to mock him, saying, 'This man began to build and was not able to finish.' Or what king, going to make war against another king, does not sit down first and consider whether he is able with ten thousand to meet him who comes against him with twenty thousand? Or else, while the other is still a great way off, he sends a delegation and asks conditions of peace. So likewise, whoever of you does not forsake all that he has cannot be My disciple. Salt is good; but if the salt has lost its flavor, how shall it be seasoned? It is neither fit for the land nor for the dunghill, but men throw it out. He who has ears to hear, let him hear!" Luke 14:25-35, NKJV

These were some of the most solemn and searching words that ever fell from Jesus' lips. And of all His upside-down statements, these were perhaps, and often still are, among the most misunderstood.

In fact, the multitudes shrank because of these radical and provocative statements. They were disappointed, as God knew they would be. Some wanted to be dazzled by miracles. Others wanted to be fed because they had heard about His wonderful miracle of feeding the five thousand. Some were hoping that He would overthrow the empire of Rome and establish His kingdom on earth.

They couldn't receive this message because they were thinking in ordinary terms instead of in kingdom terms.

Just as with Gideon, God was willing to thin the ranks because He really wanted only those who were truly committed to Him. He's simply not interested in huge crowds or personal popularity. Here He comes along and says, "Don't misunderstand what it means to follow me. This is what I'm really after. Are you willing? If not, go on home."

The Requirements of Discipleship

So often, people tend to misinterpret the meanings behind the four qualifications Jesus gave us for discipleship. Either we make them too literal: "I'm supposed to hate my mother, and I can't own so much as a pillow" or we make them laughable: "Having a crabby boss must be your cross to bear in life."

As we study the principles of discipleship from the passage we just read in Luke, it's important that we interpret them not just according to Jesus' words. We need to interpret them also in light of other Scripture and in light of Jesus' own example. Remember, this is not radical or abnormal behavior we're talking about—only what should be considered *normal Christian living*.

With this perspective in mind, let's look at the four important requirements of discipleship that Jesus Himself laid out for us twenty centuries ago.

Requirement #1: Love God more than anyone else.
Verse 26: "If anyone comes to Me and does not hate his father and mother, wife and children, brothers and sisters, yes, and His own life also, he cannot be My disciple."

Jesus is obviously not requesting that we hate our families. We know that He loved His mother and that while He was on the cross, He instructed the disciple John to take care of her. What's more, the Bible tells us over and over again that we are to love all others, including our enemies.

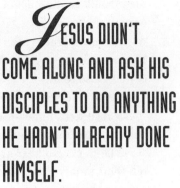

JESUS DIDN'T COME ALONG AND ASK HIS DISCIPLES TO DO ANYTHING HE HADN'T ALREADY DONE HIMSELF.

So what did Jesus mean? Well, let's look at what He did. Matthew records an incident that sheds some light on this statement.

> *While Jesus was still talking to the crowd, his mother and brothers stood outside, wanting to speak to him. Someone told him, "Your mother and brothers are standing outside, wanting to speak to you."*
>
> *He replied to him, "Who is my mother, and who are my brothers?" Pointing to his disciples, he said, "Here are my mother and my brothers. For whoever does the will of my Father in heaven is my brother and sister and mother."* Matt. 12:46-50, NIV

As Jesus was prone to do, He saw a teaching moment and took advantage of it. His family's arrival and their request to see Him was going to interrupt His work for God. Notice the phrase "While Jesus was still talking to the crowd." Jesus made a point of saying, "God's will is more important than My family. And My spiritual family, which includes those who do My Father's will, is now My first priority, even above My earthly family."

So why did Jesus use the word *hate?* The word used here is meant to indicate the opposite of love. This method of sharp contrast was a common oriental practice. Jesus was saying essentially, "If you want to be my disciple, your love for others must be like hatred in comparison with your love for God." We could retranslate this: "If you are going to be His disciple, you must love God more than anyone or anything else. Your love for Him must be so passionate, so profound, that no other love even comes close to it."

So why is this a requirement for discipleship?

Because Jesus understood that close relationships and our desire to please our families could also hinder our commitment to serve God. I often hear about new Christians who go home and tell their family that now they're going to follow Christ. Sometimes parents, friends, or others in the family oppose this. And then the temptation is strong for the new believer to say to God, "I don't want conflict here. So I'll wait until my husband or my mother changes her mind, and then I'll follow You."

If you are going to be a follower of Jesus, you are not going to get along with everyone. It's not that you shouldn't be a loving, considerate, and caring person. You should be more so. But if you are a true follower of Jesus, some people will be offended by this. They may think that now you feel you're superior to them. Or they may miss the way you used to party with them. Or they may suddenly feel less comfortable swearing up a storm when you're within hearing.

For whatever reason, we have to expect some conflict. And here's the bottom line: Either you are going to have harmony with God and friction with some people, or you are going to have harmony with people and friction with God. If there is no conflict with any person in any area of your life because of your faith, I would suggest that you consider this principle very carefully.

Remember that Jesus said,

> *Don't imagine that I came to bring peace to the earth!*
> *No, I came to bring a sword. I have come to set a man*
> *against his father, and a daughter against her mother,*
> *and a daughter-in-law against her mother-in-law. Your*
> *enemies will be right in your own household!* Matt.
> 10:34-36, NLT

Jesus knows that faith is something that can divide families. And this is how serious Jesus is about discipleship. He is saying that it may mean a conflict with loved ones. It may even lead to severing of a romantic relationship because that person doesn't want to follow the Lord with you. But this is necessary. In fact, sometimes it's that very conflict that finally brings about an unbeliever's awareness of his need for God.

Are you willing to risk conflict with someone you love in order to help God save her soul? Are you willing to follow Jesus into battle no matter who decides to stay at home?

CLOSE RELATIONSHIPS AND OUR DESIRE TO PLEASE OUR FAMILIES COULD ALSO HINDER OUR COMMITMENT TO SERVE GOD.

Requirement #2: Bear your cross. Verse 27: "And whoever does not bear his cross and come after Me cannot be My disciple."

That is a radical statement. Once again Jesus was asking His followers to do something He Himself would have to do and was planning to do literally. "Carrying his own cross, he went out to the place of the Skull (which in Aramaic is called Golgotha)" (John 19:17, NIV).

Keep in mind that this statement doesn't have nearly the same impact in our culture that it would have had upon the original hearers. Sometimes when these people went down to Jerusalem to buy food for dinner or to visit a friend, they would hear the clank-ing of armor and spot a contingent of Roman soldiers leading a man bearing his own cross. Immediately they knew that this man was going to his death. It was a shameful thing to be crucified in Christ's time. It was a long and torturous death reserved for the most hardened of criminals.

"BEAR YOUR CROSS" MEANS THE SAME THING TO EVERY MAN AND EVERY WOMAN: "BE WILLING TO DIE."

This is what the hearers of the time would have pictured, and to many the image would have been offensive. None of them would have imagined, as many people to-day are prone to do, that to bear their cross might mean something as silly as dealing with a mother-in-law who won't mind her own busi-ness.

Jesus wasn't referring to some unique trial we each have in our life. "Bear your cross" means the same thing to every man and every woman: "Be willing to die." It would have clearly indicated a spiritual call to suffering and death.

The dramatic point Jesus was trying to make here is an impor-tant principle of discipleship. He had just told us that we must love Him more than our family and friends. And then He said that we must love Him even more than we love ourselves. In fact, we must be willing to die, to surrender our very life to follow Him.

Certainly He doesn't mean we should offer ourself to be cruci-fied. But what He does mean is that we need to be ready to put to death anything in our selfish nature that keeps us from Christ. Paul put it this way:

> *Therefore, brothers, we have an obligation—but it is not to the sinful nature, to live according to it. For if you live according to the sinful nature, you will die; but if by the*

*Spirit you put to death the misdeeds of the body, you will
live, because those who are led by the Spirit of God are
sons of God."* Rom. 8:12-14, NIV

God isn't asking us to put to death anything good. We are putting to death *that which leads us to death: sin.* And ultimately, this
putting to death of our sinful impulses leads to life. Notice that
Paul says if you do this, "you will live." And in his letter to the Galatians, he wrote, "I have been crucified with Christ and I no longer live, but Christ lives in me" (Gal. 2:20, NIV).

Jesus is trying to get us to understand a key dynamic principle.
When we give up our tight grasp on our own life, we discover life
as it was meant to be lived. When you really die to yourself, you
find yourself. When you lay aside your personal goals, desires,
and ambitions, that is when God will reveal the goals, desires, and
ambitions that He has for you. Christian author A. W. Tozer once
said, "In every Christian's heart there is a cross and a throne. And
the Christian is on the throne until he puts himself on the cross. If
he refuses the cross, he remains on the throne."

Too often, we want to be saved,
but we insist that Christ do all the
dying. No cross for us. No de-
thronement. We remain king
within the little kingdom of our
soul, and we wear our tinsel
crown with all the pride of Caesar.
It's hard to lay our life down. It
feels upside down *not* to put our-
selves first. It goes against our natural impulse to pursue our selfish desires and lusts.

> *Ultimately,
> the putting to death
> of our sinful impulses
> leads to life.*

But whom do you want on the throne of your heart?

Requirement #3: Forsake all you have.
Verse 33: "Whoever of you does not forsake all that he has cannot be My disciple."

Once again Jesus drives a hard bargain. What does He mean, forsake all I own? Do I have to have the world's largest garage sale and sell everything I possess, including my kids' bikes and that brand-new home computer I got last Christmas? I'm willing to endure some conflict with family. I'm willing to die to selfish desires. But now You want my boat, Lord?

Once again, we can't take Jesus' words to their literal extreme. And yet to ignore *any* literal sense of interpretation would also be a mistake. We need to look at things from God's upside-down perspective, which always puts the spiritual before the physical. And we need to look to Jesus' life for help. In Matthew 8:19-20 we read, "Then a teacher of the law came to him and said, 'Teacher, I will follow you wherever you go.' Jesus replied, 'Foxes have holes and birds of the air have nests, but the Son of Man has no place to lay his head' " (NIV).

This is how literally Jesus lived out this principle. He had no home. We don't read about His possessing anything at all except perhaps His tunic and cloak. And yet Jesus visits Mary and Martha in *their* home, and various times the Bible instructs us to show hospitality to strangers. If Joseph of Arimathea had sold all he had, he couldn't have bought Jesus' burial tomb.

Jesus wants us to dig deep and grasp the principle behind His words. Let's understand what the phrase *forsake all you have* means. It could be literally translated "surrender your claim to, say good-bye to." How often we say things like, "We painted our house the other day." "We drove our car." We refer to these things as *ours*. "That's my husband. That's my career." But in reality, if I am a disciple, I realize that all of this is under the ownership of Jesus.

I heard the story of a woman who had been working very hard one long day and decided to reward herself with a little treat down at the local mall. She found a Mrs. Fields cookies store and ordered a whole bag of fresh hot cookies just for herself. Then she went next door to Starbucks and got herself a grande latte, half-calf, with light foam and a touch of vanilla (whatever happened to a regular cup of coffee?). She then pulled out a *USA Today* from her purse, found a nice quiet table, and sat down to enjoy her cookies and latte.

A couple of minutes later a man sat down across from her. As she was reading her paper and munching on her first cookie she heard a rustling in her cookie bag on the table. Folding down the top of her paper, she thought she saw this man's hand pull out of her bag. He popped a cookie in his mouth. She thought to herself, *Surely that isn't possible; he wouldn't just take one of my cookies.* She heard the cookie bag rustle again, and this time she caught him in the very act of swiping one of her cookies. He didn't seem concerned at all. He just reached in and took another and another.

She would eat a cookie and he would eat one, all the time with a broad smile on his face. This lady was furious, but she was afraid to confront someone who would so blatantly steal her food. Finally there was only one cookie left in the bag. They reached for it at the same time and came out of the bag, each hanging on to a half of that final cookie. Smiling again, the man broke off half and gave it to her. He then ate the other half.

The woman was so angry that she bolted up from that table and walked away in a great huff. As she walked back to her office, she opened her purse to put the newspaper in it. There was her bag of cookies! The man hadn't been eating her cookies; she'd been eating his! And he was nice enough to even share the last one with her.

We boast of our future, our possessions, our plans, our cookies. In the process of doing this we forget the passage of Scripture that says, "Do you not know that your body is the temple of the Holy Spirit who is in you, whom you have from God, and you are not your own? For you were bought at a price; therefore glorify God in your body and in your spirit, which are God's" (1 Cor. 6:19-20, NKJV).

Jesus is asking, "Are you willing to give up *anything* to follow Me? Not only must you love Me more than your family, but you must love Me more than your home, your bed, your comfort. I don't guarantee these things as part of the 'follow Me' package." This enables us to demonstrate God's love to others in a tangible way. It also reminds us that everything we have is a gift from Him.

As we've seen, the first church lived out this principle in a radical way: "All the believers were one in heart and mind. No one claimed that any of his possessions was his own, but they shared everything they had" (Acts 4:32, NIV).

Are you ready?

Requirement #4: Count the cost.

Verse 28: "For which of you, intending to build a tower, does not sit down first and count the cost, whether he has enough to finish it—lest, after he has laid the foundation, and is not able to finish, all who see it begin to mock him, saying, 'This man began to build and was not able to finish.' Or what king, going to make war against another king, does not sit down first and consider whether he is able with ten thousand to meet him who comes against him with twenty thousand?"

I wanted to address this statement of Jesus last because in many ways it is a summary of the others. He's told us the price: potential conflict with loved ones; a decision to die daily to selfish sins; and a willingness to forsake, or let go of, our claim to all our material possessions. Now He's asking us to count up these costs and decide whether or not we're willing to pay the price.

You'll notice something important here. Christ is not asking us to pay the price for salvation. That's a free gift if we repent and put our faith in Him. However, to become a true disciple, a follower who doesn't turn back but goes forward and helps to gain ground for God, we must sit down and carefully weigh our motives and our commitment.

Have you ever made an impulse purchase and bought something you didn't need? Cars are the worst. You are planning to buy a car within a certain price range. It's all you can afford. The salesman says, "Have you looked at this hot new model that came out? This baby is fast."

"No. I'm a practical person," you say. "And I could not afford that."

"Want to take it for a spin?" he asks.

"What's the point?" you ask.

He smiles big at this. "What if I were to tell you that you could drive this off the lot for the same price you would have paid for this other car you were looking at?"

> *T*O BECOME A TRUE DISCIPLE, WE MUST SIT DOWN AND CAREFULLY WEIGH OUR MOTIVES AND OUR COMMITMENT.

"I would say I'm interested." So you take it out for a test drive. It feels good. You like it. And there's that intoxicating smell of fresh new leather.

Back at the car lot you ask, "If you could get this to me for the same price . . ."

He says, "Let me talk to my manager. Just wait here."

He disappears for thirty minutes. You might imagine they're really talking about this. But you know what? He's probably just having a cup of coffee with his buddies. He is not going to take that offer to the manager. Never intended to. He's waiting for you to get even more hooked and to invest even more time.

He comes back and says, "I'm so sorry. The manager said we can't do it. But we can give it to you for this price."

It's not much less than the sticker price. But before you can think about it, before you've really counted the cost, you sign a paper that you'll probably regret for five years.

Jesus is saying, "Don't follow Me impulsively. Think about this. Count the cost. Mean it."

Why does God require this? Because He's not like some pushy used-car salesman. He won't sign you up if you don't really qualify or if you don't understand all the issues. He's looking for spiritual soldiers who are wholeheartedly committed to their mission.

Gideon didn't have to worry that one of his soldiers would turn back halfway through the attack. In the same way, God is looking for disciples who have decided to risk everything in order to follow Him into enemy territory.

Jesus set the ultimate example of counting the cost when He went to the cross. In the Gospel of John, Jesus declares, "The reason my Father loves me is that I lay down my life—only to take it up again. No one takes it from me, but I lay it down of my own accord" (John 10:17-18, NIV).

Jesus had counted the cost and made His decision. This does not mean that when the moment came to follow through, He wasn't wishing it cost less. It doesn't mean it was easy. And neither do we have to follow Christ like a bunch of robots. Sometimes it hurts to pay the price. That's a legitimate response. But it's a lot easier to pay a price that you've already decided you can afford.

Salty Salt

"Salt is good; but if the salt has lost its flavor, how shall it be seasoned? It is neither fit for the land nor for the dunghill, but men throw it out. He who has ears to hear, let him hear!" (vv. 34-35).

After stating the requirements for discipleship, Jesus made this final statement by way of explanation and warning. In Bible times, salt wasn't just another spice or something used to make popcorn taste good. It was often used to preserve food. And because they had no refrigeration, they wrapped meat in salt so that it would not putrefy and rot. Our modern equivalent would be beef jerky.

So when Jesus said, "You are the salt of the earth" in Matthew

5:13 and again in this passage, He was saying something about how we influence the world and preserve what is good. If we lose the main qualities that make us His disciples and therefore distinct and visible in the world—if we stop making a difference— we stop representing God. We're no longer salty.

Another use for salt was to stimulate thirst. If you are being a salty Christian, so to speak, your lifestyle will stimulate in others a thirst for God. They will watch you. They might laugh at you. But they will watch you and wonder, *What is it with this person? What makes her tick?*

If you are looking for a life of ease with no conflict or sacrifice, then the life of a disciple is not for you. But let me also add that if you don't want to be a disciple, then you don't want to be a true follower of Jesus Christ. A true follower naturally becomes a disciple, and the normal disciple's life looks abnormal to an unbelieving world.

> *IF YOU ARE BEING A SALTY CHRISTIAN, SO TO SPEAK, YOUR LIFESTYLE WILL STIMULATE IN OTHERS A THIRST FOR GOD.*

When we see all of this in Scripture, it's easy to say, "I believe these things." But what about when we are tested? What about when we really need to walk by faith and not by sight or feeling? What about when we need to trust God in an area where we are facing need or sickness or some other calamity?

Remember in Acts 4, when Peter and John were called before the elders and the teachers of the law and questioned? If you take only one idea away from this chapter, this would be a good one and should be the goal of every true disciple:

> *When they saw the courage of Peter and John and realized that they were unschooled, ordinary men, they were astonished and they took note that these men had been with Jesus.* Acts 4:13, NIV

Does your behavior astonish people? Is it obvious to those who speak with you that you've spent time with Jesus? Can they taste the salt?

The true tests of discipleship don't come in glorious moments. The war is ordinary, long, and sometimes quite ugly. Will you say, "Lord, I want to be like one of Gideon's three hundred. I would like to be a man or a woman who will stand in the gap for You and be Your real disciple and live an effective Christian life"?

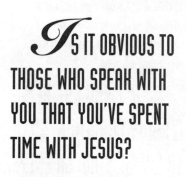

Is it obvious to those who speak with you that you've spent time with Jesus?

A little salt makes a big difference. And godly living in an ungodly situation can make a huge difference. God can do a lot with a little. It starts with you. Soon one disciple becomes two, and two become four, and four become eight, and eight become sixteen.

Evangelist John Wesley said many years ago, "Give me a hundred men who love God with all of their hearts and fear nothing but sin, and I will move the world."

I think that is still true. If we can find a few men and women who love God with all of their hearts and fear nothing but sin, we can build an army of disciples capable of turning the world upside down. We may lose a battle here and there, but we are not going to lose this war.

Remember God's exhortation: "Am I not sending you? So go in the strength you have."

THE IMPORTANCE OF "LITTLE" JOBS

Question: How does Harvest involve "the little people," not just to get the work done but as lay ministers? How do you make them feel that they're turning the world upside down by ushering?

Answer: Warren Wiersbe said, "You can never be too small for God to use, only too big."

We have ministry opportunities for everyone at Harvest, no matter what their gifts and calling are. Yet even if a person has a gift of communicating, we would not immediately place such a person in leadership.

We believe faithfulness is of the greatest importance.

We will intentionally give relatively menial tasks to people who want to serve so that we can test that faithfulness, much as Stephen and Philip waited on tables.

If they are faithful, in time they can advance to greater opportunities. If a person objects to this, it shows me that he or she does not have a true "servant's heart," which I believe is essential for effective leadership.

Even if people do not feel called to teach or preach, there are many opportunities for them to serve in ministries ranging from new-convert counseling to helping people find a parking space.

EIGHT

A READY ANSWER
Learning to Love
God's Word

HAVE YOU ever had one of those golden opportunities to share the gospel, and you really weren't prepared?

When I was young, I had a friend whose name was also Gregg. We attended elementary school together, and as we got older, we hung out, experimented with drugs, and got into trouble together.

After I became a Christian, I promised Gregg that I would not turn into a religious fanatic. "Listen," I said, "I know these Jesus freaks are weird. But don't worry. Your good buddy Greg Laurie will never become one of those weirdo Christians walking around carrying a Bible, talking to total strangers about God, wearing a cross around his neck, and saying stuff like 'Praise the Lord.' I am going to be cool about this."

Gregg seemed reassured. But, of course, I hadn't taken into account the power of the Holy Spirit in a person's life and the dramatic changes He can bring about.

One day a couple weeks later, I was walking around in Newport Beach. I wanted to get out and do something with my faith, so I had gone down there to share the gospel with whomever God might send across my path. Who do I run into but Gregg!

I hadn't seen my friend since our last conversation. And here I was with a big Bible in my hand and a cross around my neck. We started talking. And before I could catch myself, I said, "Praise the Lord."

Gregg looked at me, and I looked at him. We both started laughing. I had become one of those crazy Christians.

I said, "I know this looks weird, but I have been on both sides of the fence now. I know the way that you think, because that is how I thought for my whole life up to this point. But now I have seen what God can do. And, Gregg, I've got to tell you, Jesus Christ is real."

As I started witnessing to Gregg, he appeared to be listening and seemed open. I was getting excited, feeling sure that I was making progress. Then suddenly another guy came up and joined us. He'd seen me walk up to Gregg and had been listening to our conversation. He happened to own a "head shop" nearby, which is what we used to call stores that sold drug paraphernalia. "I have a few questions for you," he said.

"Sure," I answered. *Not a problem,* I thought. *I have been a Christian for a couple weeks now. Fire away.*

He proceeded to direct four or five pretty tough questions my way. Today I can't even remember what they were. All I remember is that I was dumbfounded. I didn't have a clue as to how to answer. Meanwhile, my good friend Gregg kept turning to me and saying, "Yeah, Greg, what about that? He's right, why does God do that? Why doesn't God do this?"

I was ashamed and embarrassed. But worst of all I felt that I had let the Lord down. I made a commitment that day to study the Bible, to know what it had to say so I would not be caught in that position again. I am not suggesting that now I have the answer to every question or that I can resolve any difficulty. But I realized then and there that I wanted to equip myself with God's Word so I could become an increasingly better witness for Christ.

A Matter of Life and Death

In the previous chapter we saw that a "learning church" is filled with true disciples—those who are trying to become like Christ based on what He said and what He did. Now I want to talk with you about imitating Christ by becoming a student of Scripture. The word *disciple* can actually be translated "learner."

Keep in mind, however, that the kind of learner that makes a true disciple is not just a student who listens passively. A disciple is someone who is completely intent on watching and listening to his teacher and who is drinking in every word with an intense desire to apply what he's learning. The early church studied the Scriptures wholeheartedly. Remember what we read in Acts 2:42: "And they continued steadfastly in the apostles' doctrine and fellowship, in the breaking of bread, and in prayers" (NKJV). Paul told Timothy, "Devote yourself to the public reading of Scripture, to preaching and to teaching" (1 Tim. 4:13, NIV).

Now at first glance, studying the Bible steadfastly or preaching the Bible in church or some other public venue doesn't sound too upside down. But you know what? That's not always happening in churches and among Christians. And it's definitely not what's happening in the world in general.

The Bible has been used to decorate coffee tables, to wave in the air while preaching, to put your hand on while taking an oath, to look spiritual on a nightstand, or to record the family tree. It has been read as great literature or a history text. The Bible is used for all these things every day.

But to use the Bible as a basis for your life choices, to desire to read it as you desire food to sustain you physically, to have an appetite for it so strong that when you don't read it, you feel empty, to believe that every word of it applies to you somehow, to try to obey it every day, to learn and to teach it all you can . . . that's definitely upside-down behavior, even in our "Christian" subculture.

I would be so bold as to say that if you know someone who

reads the Bible this way, that person's life does not look ordinary. You can tell at a glance that something is radically different about that person.

As a pastor I've been given clear direction from God as to what I should be doing. Paul said to Timothy, "Preach the word! Be ready in season and out of season. Convince, rebuke, exhort, with all longsuffering and teaching" (2 Tim. 4:2, NKJV). In the original language there is an urgency here, just as there is an urgency in the passages about evangelizing. Paul is essentially saying, "Preach the Word with alertness, with carefulness, with insistence. With passion."

PREACH THE WORD WITH ALERTNESS, WITH CAREFULNESS, WITH INSISTENCE, WITH PASSION.

But this command is not just for me as a pastor. It is for all of us as we take God's Word to the world. We should all be urgent about the Bible. We should treat this message as a matter of life and death.

I travel by plane quite a bit, and I have heard a few hundred times the speech the flight attendants give about safety and seat belts and oxygen masks. (Isn't it disconcerting how they quip so breezily, "In the event of a water landing . . ." as if this would constitute only a slight shift in plans?) I usually just flip through magazines while they make these announcements. I note where the emergency exits are, and then I go on with what I'm doing.

But what if the plane were actually going down? What if I knew that I had twenty minutes before impact, and the flight attendants gave that announcement one more time? I would not merely listen carefully; I would be frantically studying every word of that safety card for myself.

Remember the story in chapter 4 about Andrew Meekin? Christians who are really living an upside-down life for Christ approach evangelism as if the plane were going down every day.

And you know what? They also study the Bible *as if their life depended on knowing what it contains.* Because in many ways it does.

Unfortunately many churches and individuals just aren't studying, preaching, and learning the Bible this way. It amazes me how many preachers have lost sight of this urgency. Just turn on the TV on Sunday mornings. Go channel surfing and listen carefully. It's rare to hear someone actually speak from the Bible. And in many churches it's rare to hear the pastor say, "Please turn in your Bible to . . ." I have to confess that the sweetest sound to my ears is when I say this phrase and then hear the responsive rustle of Bible pages all through the sanctuary.

It's hard to understand this lack of passion for the Bible. What's gone wrong? Why are so many of us failing to turn those pages, preach from those pages, and feed our soul from them?

The rest of the passage Paul wrote to Timothy provides some clues. It continues,

> *For the time will come when they will not endure sound doctrine, but according to their own desires, because they have itching ears, they will heap up for themselves teachers; and they will turn their ears away from the truth, and be turned aside to fables.* 2 Tim. 4:3-4, NKJV

I want you to notice the bold parts of the above verses, because I believe that this time has come. And I believe these verses point to the three biggest reasons we have turned away from our love for the Word. We have spoiled appetites; we think we need more than the Bible; and we have ears that want to be tickled instead of taught.

1. We have spoiled appetites.

I was talking with a man back in North Carolina some time ago who is an expert in so-called church growth. He told me about another pastor who had started a church for Gen Xers.

I said, "Tell me; I'm really interested. What distinguishes a church that is targeted toward Xers or baby busters?"

He said, "For starters, they have televisions lining the walls on both sides of the sanctuary all the way from the front to the back."

"What's the purpose of that?"

"Well, the pastor speaks for about ten minutes, and then they break and have a video. Then he speaks a little more. Then another video. They do this because they know that people's attention span is too short to listen to the pastor for too long."

I think this is dangerous. Remember the phrase from Timothy? "They will not endure sound doctrine." Apparently these folks will not endure any kind teaching for more than ten minutes at a time.

What's happening here? Has our attention span shrunk since the first century? I don't think so. I think we've lost our ability to endure Bible teaching because we've have had our appetite spoiled by sweet stuff and fluff in place of the meat of the Word. The simple fact that we would have to *endure* teaching versus *desire* teaching is a bad sign. We *endure* liver and onions (at least I do).

People will develop an appetite for what you feed them. *Yet the fact that people develop an appetite for what they're served over time doesn't mean that they're consuming what their spirit is truly hungry for.*

I believe people are deeply hungry for the Bible. I think they want to hear what the Bible has to say. When they come to church, they don't expect the pastor to be a pop psychologist or a comedian or a political activist. They actually expect a preacher to preach from the Bible. Whether they are Gen Xers or boomers, everyone wants to know what the meaning of life is. Everybody wants to know God. And the answers are found in the Scriptures. We are going to have to learn how to sit down, slow down, and learn to enjoy the feast that's in the Bible.

2. We think we need more than the Word.
One undisputed leader of the church growth movement has said something I think is surprising. "If somebody has been sexually molested, if someone has grown up in the home of an alcoholic father, if someone has been beaten as a child, there are some deep psychological wounds that have to be carefully treated by trained Christian counselors before these wounded people can thoroughly appropriate the promises and precepts of Scripture." He closes: "Traditional preaching alone is not enough to restore many people to wholeness."

*W*HEN SEEKERS COME TO CHURCH, THEY DON'T EXPECT THE PASTOR TO BE A POP PSYCHOLOGIST OR A COMEDIAN OR A POLITICAL ACTIVIST.

I understand that this pastor is being sensitive to the deep wounds of people. However, I disagree with the idea that the Word preached is inadequate to restore people to wholeness. I guess part of the problem has to do with how we interpret "wholeness" and whether or not that is our goal.

Notice the phrase from 2 Timothy: "according to their own desires." Somewhere along the way we got the idea that the goal of a Christian is personal well-being. We desire healthy egos and high self-esteem and peace with our past, etc. We no longer believe in the power of salvation to make us new. Consider what Christ says: "My grace is sufficient for you, for my power is made perfect in weakness" (2 Cor. 12:9, NIV).

This subtle idea that the Bible is not sufficient has crept into our churches, and as a result we're neglecting the study of the Bible. Instead, many churches lean more and more heavily on books, philosophies, and small groups that focus on making us well and happy rather than on how we can live abundantly by denying ourselves for Christ.

Do you want healing? Everything you need is in the Bible. Psalm 107:20-21 says, "He sent His word and healed them, and delivered them from their destructions. Oh, that men would give thanks to the Lord for His goodness, and for His wonderful works to the children of men!" (NKJV).

The gospel preached is sufficient for you. Listen to Paul:

> When I came to you, brothers, I did not come with eloquence or superior wisdom as I proclaimed to you the testimony about God. For I resolved to know nothing while I was with you except Jesus Christ and him crucified. I came to you in weakness and fear, and with much trembling. My message and my preaching were not with wise and persuasive words, but with a demonstration of the Spirit's power, so that your faith might not rest on men's wisdom, but on God's power. 1 Cor. 2:1-5, NIV

OPERATING ACCORDING TO HIS UPSIDE-DOWN PRINCIPLES WILL WORK FOR YOU NO MATTER WHAT YOUR PAST OR HOW DEEP YOUR PAIN.

If you need counseling, get it. Just make sure it is biblically sound. If you need medical attention, by all means, seek it! However, don't forget for a moment that the ultimate healer is God. And His ways are not always like ours. He works through our weaknesses. He shines through our cracked parts. In fact, He prefers to work through people who let Him use their brokenness rather than focusing all their attention on becoming "whole."

His Word is where the real answers to life are found. And operating according to His upside-down principles will work for you no matter what your past or how deep your pain.

3. We have itching ears.

When Paul mentions to Timothy that people will have "itching ears," he is using a phrase that means "an itch for novelty." Another translation is "looking for spicy bits of information."

This is a perfect description of our culture. We are seeing an explosion of bizarre and aberrant philosophies and teachings today under the banner of "spirituality."

Why are people always surprised to discover that there are spiritual forces at work in the world? This stuff has much of society absolutely fascinated. Just go down to your local bookstore at the mall, and you will see what I'm talking about: dozens of weird, bizarre books dealing with all sorts of spiritual, novel topics—none of them coming from a Christian worldview. All of

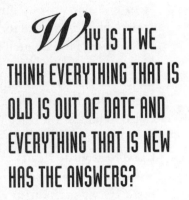

WHY IS IT WE THINK EVERYTHING THAT IS OLD IS OUT OF DATE AND EVERYTHING THAT IS NEW HAS THE ANSWERS?

them offer to titillate the curious who have itching ears.

But here is the problem. This desire to be tickled by spiritual mumbo jumbo is happening in the church as well. We are itching for new experiences. And we are even willing to disguise our penchant by cloaking it in a spiritual quest of some kind. Some will say, "It's a new move of the Spirit. We want a new thing from the Lord. Have you heard about . . . ?"

This reminds me of the mentality of the people on Mars Hill in Athens when Paul went to preach to them. These people believed in and would embrace just about anything remotely spiritual. And in Acts 17:21 we read, "All the Athenians and the foreigners who lived there spent their time doing nothing but talking about and listening to the latest ideas" (NIV).

We want something new. We don't want the old Bible stuff. Why is it we think everything that is old is antiquated and out of date and everything that is new has the answers?

I like what God says in Jeremiah: "Thus says the Lord: 'Stand in the ways and see, and ask for the old paths, where the good way is, and walk in it; then you will find rest for your souls'" (Jer. 6:16, NKJV). The old paths are the words of God, and we need to return to them, learn them, and preach them. If it is "new," it isn't true. If it is true, it isn't new.

This is not to say that God can't take His Word and make it fresh and new to our life. But when Paul said, "Preach the word," he didn't intend for me to preach politics, psychology, or social issues. He didn't tell me to preach morality in and of itself. He meant for me to preach God's Word, no matter what the topic—as clearly, honestly, and thoroughly as possible. I'm called to teach, not to tickle itching ears. And you in the pew are called to hunger for teaching.

Good Reasons to Read
So often we think of reading or preaching the Word as a Christian duty we perform so we can check it off our list of things good Christians do. But we truly need to study the Bible for more reasons than we realize.

Reading the Bible is kind of like exercising. The doctor says we need to exercise, so we reluctantly make our way down to the gym. But six weeks into it, we're not thinking anymore about what the doctor said. We want to go because we've discovered how many aspects of our life are improved by exercising.

The greatest reason to learn and to preach the Bible is so that we are all better equipped to turn the world upside down even when challenged by difficult questions from guys like the one I encountered while witnessing to my friend Gregg. But a great ability to evangelize is just one reason to read.

Here are five other important reasons why you will want to continue to study the Bible once you get started. And why you who are pastors need to keep preaching the Word to your people.

1. The Bible helps you learn theology (right ideas about God).
I make it a point to teach Bible-based theology on many Sunday mornings at my church. I want us all to have the right ideas about God and to have a grid that we can examine things by so we know what we believe and as a result know what we don't believe.

I've heard people say proudly, "I don't have any theology. I just love Jesus!" But if you have no theology, how can you share the gospel clearly? We all have a theology. We all make assumptions, either based on the Word or not, about how God works in the world. As C. S. Lewis once put it, "If you do not listen to theology, that will not mean that you have no ideas about God. It will mean that you will have a lot of wrong ones."

When we become not just lovers of the Word but students of the Word, we base our theology on the truth, and we obey God. Paul said to Timothy, "Do your best to present yourself to God as one approved, a workman who does not need to be ashamed and who correctly handles the word of truth" (2 Tim. 2:15, NIV). A wonderful place to start would be with *The New Believer's Bible*. It contains hundreds of notes on subjects ranging from the deity of Christ to how to pray effectively.

Remember when Jesus was tempted by Satan in the desert? Satan used Scripture outside its proper context, and Jesus answered him by using Scripture correctly. If you have no understanding of theology, then when Satan tries to confuse you by using the Word of God wrongly, you won't be equipped for combat. Study the Word, learn how it all works together, and you will be ready to say to Satan, "Scripture also says . . ."

> *IF YOU DO NOT LISTEN TO THEOLOGY, THAT WILL NOT MEAN THAT YOU HAVE NO IDEAS ABOUT GOD. IT WILL MEAN THAT YOU WILL HAVE A LOT OF WRONG ONES.*

2. *The Bible prepares you to recognize false teaching.*

You can try to be an expert on every weird, crazy concept that comes down the pike. But the best thing is to know the Bible so well that when you hear something, you can say, "No. That's not right because the Bible says this. That couldn't be true because the Bible says this. That's exactly right because Scripture says this."

The story is told of an inspector who worked for England's Scotland Yard in the counterfeit department. It was his job to distinguish false currency from the genuine. So someone asked, "Well, you must spend a lot of time handling counterfeit money." He said, "No, actually I don't. I spend so much time handling the real thing that I can immediately detect the counterfeit." That's the best way.

In the book of Acts we read of those who lived in Berea and had the privilege of hearing the great apostle Paul preach. Now, I have to be honest with you, if I heard Paul preach, I probably wouldn't check him out according to Scripture. This is *Paul* after all. This is the man who wrote a good portion of the New Testament. I would just kick back and take it all in.

But the Bible tells us, "Now the Bereans were of more noble character than the Thessalonians, for they received the message with great eagerness and examined the Scriptures every day to see if what Paul said was true" (Acts 17:11, NIV). This should be the model for all believers.

Now, of course, when we read his writings in the Bible, we don't have to question whether or not these writings are right. Those are inspired by God. But these people scrutinized the Scriptures to see if what was being taught to them checked out. And if these people checked out the words of Paul the apostle, how much more should we check out our preachers and so-called apostles and prophets today?

John wrote, "Dear friends, do not believe everyone who claims to speak by the Spirit. You must test them to see if the spirit they have comes from God. For there are many false prophets in the world" (1 John 4:1, NLT).

I encourage anyone to do that with me. Never accept what I say because I say it. Who am I? A fallible person. Make sure that what I say agrees with what the Scripture teaches. If you have a good working knowledge of the Bible, you will be able to detect false teaching quickly.

3. *The Bible is spiritual food for your soul.*

When you get up in the morning, what is the first thing you think about? The Bible? If you do, I tip my hat to you. But when I get up in the morning, the first thing I think about isn't the Bible or church or ministry or even my wife. I usually think about food. That's just human nature. *I must eat soon.*

Now let's try to broaden that idea to include spiritual food. If I am going to neglect a meal because my schedule is so hectic, wouldn't it be great if I neglected a physical meal and made time for the Word of God instead of neglecting the

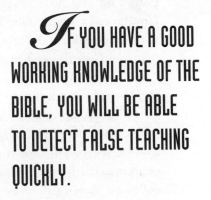

IF YOU HAVE A GOOD WORKING KNOWLEDGE OF THE BIBLE, YOU WILL BE ABLE TO DETECT FALSE TEACHING QUICKLY.

Word of God to eat that physical meal? I love what Job said: "I have treasured the words of His mouth more than my necessary food" (Job 23:12, NKJV).

Experts tell us that we are what we eat. That's also the case spiritually. If the right spiritual ingredients, which can be found only in the Bible, are missing, then we are spiritually deficient and malnourished. As a result, we are spiritually weak and vulnerable.

If we feed on God's Word, we will develop an appetite for it. And every day we will say with the psalmist, "As the deer pants for streams of water, so my soul pants for you, O God. My soul thirsts for God, for the living God. When can I go and meet with God?" (Ps. 42:1-2, NIV).

This is how Jesus felt about God's Word, and this is the attitude we should imitate if we want to be disciples: "Man does not live on bread alone, but on every word that comes from the mouth of God" (Matt. 4:4, NIV).

4. The Bible enables you to know God's will.

So many of us spend hours praying, "God, show me your will."

But the greatest key to knowing God's will in almost any situation is knowing what the Word says. We need to base our decisions on biblical principles as well as on the common sense God gives us—what God speaks to us personally, as well as what He speaks to us through those we respect.

I would like to say that every day God speaks to me audibly. After I wake up and think of food, God whispers, "Good morning, Greg; how are you?"

"I'm good, Lord. How are things up there?"

"Really great. Greg, here is the plan for today. And here is My will for you. I want you to leave the house at 7:46. When you get to the office, I want you to call this person."

But He doesn't. So how do I know God's will? I read the Word, and I operate by faith on biblical principles. When I come to a difficult situation or choice, I ask myself, *What biblical principles can guide me here?*

What does the Bible say? Then that is what I will do.

A lot of us are looking for this mystical, supernatural thing to happen, a loud voice from heaven declaring, "This is My will. . . ." But reading the Bible is what helps us to have the mind of Christ. It is how we can get our brain into a mode where everything goes through the grid of scriptural thinking. That is primarily how we are going to know the mind of Christ—and the will of God.

5. The Bible is one way God speaks to you personally.
After Jesus was crucified, two discouraged followers were traveling on the Emmaus road. They were devastated. They had thought Jesus was going to establish a physical kingdom and overthrow the tyranny of Rome, but instead He'd gotten Himself killed.

Now, He had told them repeatedly, "I am going to die. I am going to rise again on the third day." But they didn't understand this.

As they were walking along and talking, a stranger joined them, and they welcomed Him to walk along with them. They started to converse. He asked, "What are you talking about?"

They said, "Haven't you heard about all of the things concerning Jesus of Nazareth?"

"What things?"

And they began to tell Him all of the things that had happened. "And besides all of this, it's the third day since He was crucified."

He said, "You fools and slow of heart to believe" (see Luke 24:25). And the Bible says that beginning with Moses and the prophets, He opened to them all the things in the Scriptures concerning Himself. As He spoke, they listened.

When He acted as though He was going to go farther than they, the two people insisted, "Oh no. Stay with us." They sat down, and when the stranger broke the bread, their eyes were opened spiritually, and they realized it was the Lord. Immediately He disappeared from their midst.

I love this next statement. They said, "Did not our heart burn within us while He talked with us on the road, and while He opened the Scriptures to us?" (Luke 24:32, NKJV).

We all need a good case of spiritual heartburn. We will have that when Jesus Christ speaks to us personally through His Word.

Martin Luther said, "The Bible is alive. It speaks to me. It has feet. It runs after me. It has hands. It lays hold of me." Isn't that what we want? For God to speak with us and run after us and lay hold of us? He does that through the Word.

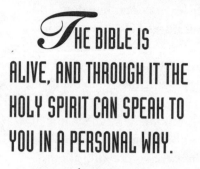

The Bible is not just words on a page. Its words are alive, and through it the Holy Spirit can speak to you in a personal way. You're reading along, and suddenly you feel Christ highlighting a key point or speaking to your sorrow through a psalm. The Bible is a key part of our personal conversation with God. Get into the Word of God. And let the Word of God get into you.

PASTOR TO PASTOR

Five Ways to See If God's Word Is in Your Word

MEASURE CONTENT. Ask yourself: Are my stories and observations helping to illuminate the Bible passage, or is the Bible there simply to help justify the importance of my stories? Is the Bible my swimming pool, where I spend the most time, or is it simply my diving board?

2. MEASURE COVERAGE. Ask yourself: If my church were a lawn and my Bible teaching fertilizer, would my lawn be turning evenly green or a weird pattern of stripes and burn holes? We should be striving to preach the whole Word as thoroughly as possible over the course of time. Paul said he had not failed "to declare the whole counsel of God." Could you make that same claim?

3. MEASURE CONSUMPTION. Ask yourself: What kind of food is my church consuming? Are the people growing

mature on the meat of the Word, or are most of them still eating out of the blender? If you looked at a sampling of your sermons, would you find enough to feed a hungry church family? Are you explaining complex ideas and cutting them into smaller pieces for new believers? For the "grown-ups," have you offered further reading ideas, posed challenging questions, and gone beyond the basics of salvation?

4. MEASURE CREATIVITY.   Ask yourself: Am I doing justice to the Bible's amazing stories and surprising insights and principles? Or am I putting people to sleep with the truth—just giving them what they expect? Jesus communicated Bible truth through stories that were full of color, smells, and life. The Bible isn't boring, but as one old-time seminary professor used to say, one proof of the inspiration of Scripture is that it has withstood so much poor preaching.

5. MEASURE YOUR CONCERN.   Ask yourself: Do I preach the Word as if I'm on that airplane that's going down? Martin Lloyd-Jones described this urgency as "logic on fire." Some have the fire with no logic, or content. Others have the content but no passion. We need to combine the two.

SIGNS OF LOVE

Question: What are key indicators in a church that a love of God's Word is alive and well?

Answer: For starters, when you see people coming to church with their Bibles, that's an indication that things are on the right track. There have been times when I have spoken at other churches, and I will often begin my message with the words "Let's turn in our Bibles to . . ." It's always a cause for concern when people get that blank look on their faces because they don't have Bibles with them.

Second, you will sense an anticipation and eagerness to get into Scripture. I believe there is a need for genuine Spirit-directed preaching today, but I also believe there is a need for genuine Spirit-directed listening. Listening not only with our head but with our heart, having an openness to receive God's Word. First Peter 2:2 says, "You must crave pure spiritual milk so that you can grow into the fullness of your salvation. Cry out for this nourishment as a baby cries for milk" (NLT). We must come not only to hear the Word, but we should come also with a desire to apply it.

Third, if there is a love of God's Word in a church, I also think you will see this reflected in people's desire to attend other Bible studies during the week in addition to Sunday-morning services.

NINE

PASSING IT ON
Making Disciples
of Others

I BECAME a Christian in high school. But even as I prayed to receive Jesus Christ into my life, I was unceremoniously interrupted by the ringing of the bell to go to fifth period. No one told me that I needed to read the Bible. No one told me that I should pray or go to church. No one gave me any materials to read, much less a Bible.

For a few days I was in sort of a spiritual no-man's-land. Suddenly I didn't feel as comfortable hanging out with my old friends. Yet I didn't feel that I fit in with the Christians either.

I felt isolated until God directed a young man named Mark to come and take me under his wing. Mark had noticed me at the Bible study on the day I turned my life over to Christ. He approached me and said simply, "I would like to encourage you and take you to church with me."

I was more than open. Mark took me to Calvary Chapel, and he began to help me grow spiritually. He taught me how to read the Bible, and we prayed together. Mark wasn't a great Bible scholar or especially gifted to teach. But he was the first actual Christian I came to know personally who could model for me what it was to be a disciple of Jesus and to be a discipler of others.

Beyond New Birth

Several chapters back we examined the great commission. We saw that it is God's assignment for all of us and that we need to care about evangelizing people who haven't yet found God. Now there's a key point that we should revisit. Somewhere along the line we in the church have separated evangelism from discipleship. But the two are inseparably linked.

Though one applies to Christians and one to non-Christians, evangelizing and discipling are, and should be, part of the same process. Jesus said, "Go therefore and *make disciples* of all the nations, baptizing them in the name of the Father and of the Son and of the Holy Spirit, teaching them to observe all things that I have commanded you" (Matt. 28:19-20, NKJV; italics added).

What exactly does it mean to make disciples? Part of verse 20 defines it for us: teaching people to observe all things that He has commanded. Simply put, it means to show others how to obey what Jesus has taught us. To disciple people is to live out our faith, to teach it by word, and to model it by example. We seek to lead people to Christ and then, to the best of our ability, help them get up on their feet and become spiritually mature.

Would we ever consider abandoning a newborn baby in the hopes that he will find what it needs in order to grow?

In Colossians 1:28 Paul puts it this way: "So, naturally, we proclaim Christ! We warn everyone we meet, and we teach everyone we can, all that we know about him, so that we may bring every man up to his full maturity in Christ" (Phillips).

In a previous chapter we talked about what it means to become a true upside-down disciple of Christ. But a key part of being disciples ourselves is to be involved in making yet other disciples. And if Jesus is our ultimate example of a disciple, we should be trying to imitate His careful nurturing of His own followers.

We can also see discipleship as a key part of God's reproductive plan for His kingdom. Of course, we don't actually create Christian "babies"; God does that. But you might say that we assist at the birth. Would we ever consider abandoning a newborn baby in the hopes that he will find what it needs in order to grow? You wouldn't do that any more than a doctor would deliver a baby and then immediately give the little tyke a box of Pampers, put him out on the sidewalk, and say, "OK, son, God bless you. It has been good to be with you for this short time. Now go make something of yourself!" We need to take great care to nurture, protect, and guide those we lead to Christ.

Saul's Story

Did you ever notice in Scripture that even the apostles needed discipling? And often more than one person participated. Just as it may take more than one person to bring someone to the point of following Christ, we all have a part to play in discipling others so that they can in turn go out and shake the world for Christ.

God gives some great examples through the story of Saul. After Saul's conversion, many believers were uncertain about whether or not his Christianity was real. This is understandable. Saul was a dangerous man and had been a relentless persecutor of the church. Some people worried that Saul was pulling some kind of trick. What if he only claimed to be a Christian so that he could infiltrate the ranks of believers, get all their names, and have them arrested?

Having Saul become a Christian would be like hearing today that Saddam Hussein or Howard Stern or Marilyn Manson had turned his life over to Christ. The world, and even many in the church, might doubt that for a while.

In Saul's case, God sent a man named Ananias to help out. He said, "I want you to go and visit Saul. He is your brother, and he is in prayer."

Ananias must have been shocked to hear this. *Are we talking about the same Saul here?* He replied to God, "I have heard many reports about this man and all the harm he has done to your saints in Jerusalem. And he has come here with authority from the chief priests to arrest all who call on your name" (Acts 9:13-14, NIV).

Isn't it humorous how we think we're giving God a news flash? But the Lord replied to Ananias, "Go! This man is my chosen instrument to carry my name before the Gentiles and their kings and before the people of Israel. I will show him how much he must suffer for my name" (Acts 9:15-16, NIV).

Once again God's plans run counter to what we would do. God chose an enemy at present to become His "chosen instrument."

*B*ECAUSE ANANIAS WAS OBEDIENT, HIS INVESTMENT IN THE APOSTLE PAUL WOULD BE MULTIPLIED A MILLION TIMES OVER FOR CENTURIES TO COME.

Fortunately Ananias was obedient, even if he didn't fully understand God's purposes. He went and found Saul, called him brother, baptized him, and took the time to pray with and encourage him (see Acts 9:10-19).

Are you willing to disciple any person God sends your way—or sends you to help? Even the most unlikely of candidates or those you don't appear to have much in common with? Ananias's role in Saul's life can't be overestimated. You never know who you are discipling or what God has planned for that person. Because Ananias was obedient, his investment in the apostle Paul would be multiplied a million times over for centuries to come.

Excuses, Excuses

The most common excuse we give for not being actively involved in discipling others is that we don't feel qualified. We don't know enough about the Bible, and we're sure there's someone else out there more spiritually mature who has a gift for this kind of thing.

Besides, if we happen to be parents, we're discipling our own kids at home, aren't we? And those people who need discipling can always go to a Bible study or something, can't they?

But if we are brutally honest, often the reason we don't disciple others is that we're not living the Christian life we know we ought to be. We don't want to disciple others because we're going through the motions ourselves. Why set ourselves up to fail or to expose our inconsistencies to others? I mean, we don't want to cause a brother or sister to stumble. Maybe later, when we're not struggling so much ourselves . . . down the road. . . . But wait a second. Let's look at what Saul did after Ananais went to him.

> *Saul spent several days with the disciples in Damascus. At once he began to preach in the synagogues that Jesus is the Son of God. All those who heard him were astonished and asked, "Isn't he the man who raised havoc in Jerusalem among those who call on this name? And hasn't he come here to take them as prisoners to the chief priests?" Yet Saul grew more and more powerful and baffled the Jews living in Damascus by proving that Jesus is the Christ.* Acts 9:19-22, NIV

Notice that Saul didn't say, "Wow! I've been such a terrible example. I'm such a bad person; I can't possibly go out there yet and proclaim Jesus or teach others that He is the Christ!"

Instead, he immediately began to pass on to others the Good News he had received. And what happened? People were shocked; some probably snickered in disbelief. But this, too, was part of God's plan. If a very good and righteous person had begun to proclaim Christ, no one would have thought much about it. *But Saul's testimony was amazing proof of God's power to dramatically change any person's life, no matter what he or she has done.*

Disciple Making Is the Natural Outlet for a Disciple

What I really want you to see is what happened to Paul himself as a result of his efforts. We're told that he "grew more and more powerful." Paul thrived spiritually because he was doing what he was supposed to do—even though he was technically the least qualified to do it.

Maybe you're at a place in your Christian walk where you simply feel that you're in a spiritual desert. You read the Bible, and you think, *It's just not speaking to me the way it used to.* You come to church and think, *This is all good stuff, but I feel as if I've heard a lot of these things before.* You're trying your best to love God and live the Christian life, but the fire that once burned in your soul feels as if it's smoldered down to a smoking log.

Guess what? You probably don't need to attend more Bible studies. You may not even need to read more Christian books or go to more church services. The real problem may be that you don't have an outlet for what you are taking in. And if you do not have an outlet for spiritual truths in your life, you are going to lose heat and energy. You can keep blowing on those coals all you want. But what you really need is to share what you know with others; then your fire will grow.

The truths that God gives us are designed to be passed on. And when we give away what God has given to us, it actually *replenishes* our spiritual supply!

Have you ever discipled anyone? Have you ever taken a new believer under your wing and helped her along? Then you know, or at least you remember, that when you give your life away to disciple others, you get back so much more. It sounds cliché, but it's true. The new believers need our wisdom, knowledge, and experience. But we need them, too! We need their zeal, spark, and childlike simplicity of faith.

When you have a child, you begin to see things through a child's eyes again. As you watch a toddler discover ice cream for the first time, you're reminded about how wonderful and cold and creamy and amazing it is. That's why it's so fun to watch a child see the ocean for the first time. Or walk on sand or pick up snow. If you can see something through the eyes of a child, it can be like being a child all over again. And if you can see things through the eyes of a new believer, it can reignite you spiritually.

That's why, for our sake as well as theirs, we need to be involved in making new disciples. It's all a basic part of God's process of spreading His gospel. And all of us can do this. It doesn't have to entail knowing the Bible front to back. It may be as simple as inviting a new believer out to coffee after a Bible study. You may be discipling people right now and not even know it.

> *I*F YOU DON'T HAVE AN OUTLET FOR SPIRITUAL TRUTHS, YOU ARE GOING TO LOSE HEAT AND ENERGY. WHAT YOU REALLY NEED IS TO SHARE WHAT YOU KNOW WITH OTHERS.

Real Needs of New Believers

OK, so you're ready to start discipling others or to learn more about the process. Where do you start? What do young believers *really* need?

They need love and support to feel comfortable in church.
A lot of people who are raised in the church one day make their commitment to Christ and continue to attend that same church. They already know their way around.

But many, many people are new Christians like I was. They don't have a clue as to what's going on in church—why church is necessary or how to get the most out of it. For all they know, the number flashing on the monitor during the service is somebody's guess for how many days till Christ comes back instead of a signal to parents that their child needs them in the nursery.

We have a ministry for new believers called the Discipleship Team. The people in this group take up where the new-convert counselors leave off. Their objective is to help new believers adjust and get settled in our church. There is a lot of lingo and terminology they may be hearing for the first time, and we have found that what they really need is a friend.

I am so thankful that at Harvest Christian Fellowship we have so many people who come to us from an unchurched background. But I'm also aware of what this means to them. They are really in need of someone who will become a friend to them and say, "How are you doing? Have you met anybody? Do you have any friends? Have you been to church here before? Did your child find his class OK?"

On a deeper level, think of some of these young kids who come from broken homes. Maybe one or both parents are not involved in their lives. They decide to follow Jesus. Here you are, a Christian couple. How wonderful it would be if you could take that young one in and become almost like spiritual foster parents. Show them what it is to love one another. Show them what it is to have a stable home. You can influence a child for the rest of his life.

They need help and encouragement to
understand the Bible correctly.
One couple mentioned in Acts, Aquila and Priscilla, illustrate how we should help new converts. We read in Acts 18 how a man by the name of Apollos was filled with enthusiasm for the Lord. However, he had a few doctrinal problems. So Aquila and

Priscilla took him into their home. The Bible says they explained the way of God to him more accurately. As a result, Apollos became even more effective in what God had called him to do.

Remember the parable of the sower? The first thing that Satan will try to do when someone receives the Word is to come and pluck it away. How crucial it is for us to care for the spiritual ground of those souls who receive Christ! I can't overstate how important it is for you to be willing to disciple one of these believers, helping to snatch back, to hold firm, what Satan would distort or try to uproot.

*B*E WILLING TO DISCIPLE A NEW BELIEVER, HELPING TO SNATCH BACK, TO HOLD FIRM, WHAT SATAN WOULD DISTORT OR TRY TO UPROOT.

One of the simplest ways to provide this opportunity is through home Bible studies. At Harvest we have many such opportunities through the week. Here, older Christians can mingle with new Christians, and the wonderful process of discipleship can take place. Of course, these studies only function because of those who are willing to take the time to disciple others. I'm aware that a Bible study can turn into a gab session or a debate-a-thon. How important it is for us to take seriously the teaching of simple, basic truths in the Word.

One ministry that has been very effective at our church is something that we call the men's and women's Bible study fellowship. These groups simply meet and go through a book of the Bible together. Often there's a beneficial dynamic to having men meet together and women meet together. There will be a time of teaching, and then they will break into smaller groups and discuss what they have heard. A facilitator helps to keep the discussion on track.

This is a simple but great way to provide discipleship for new believers as well as to provide an opportunity for church members to grow in their teaching and discipling skills.

They need to see a Christian life in action.
New believers can get only so much information from a pulpit. What they need is to see God's principles at work in real life on a day-to-day basis. How does a Christian behave at work? How does a Christian behave when he drives? How does a Christian man treat his wife and children? Or how about single Christians? How do single Christians relate to members of the opposite sex? How does a Christian spend his or her free time? That is why Paul reminds Timothy: "Now you have observed my teaching, my conduct, my aim in life and my faith" (2 Tim. 3:10, paraphrased).

They need your help to mature in their own gifts and ministries.
John said his greatest joy was in seeing his children walk in the truth (3 John 1:4). As an evangelist I love to see people make that initial commitment to follow Christ. Yet as a pastor I find great joy in seeing people continuing in the faith and even leading others to faith.

NEW BELIEVERS CAN GET ONLY SO MUCH INFORMATION FROM A PULPIT. WHAT THEY NEED IS TO SEE GOD'S PRINCIPLES AT WORK IN REAL LIFE ON A DAY-TO-DAY BASIS.

Almost all of our associate pastors at Harvest either came to Christ in one of our services or began attending as very young believers. And I could cite many examples of people who have come to faith at our church and have not only continued in the faith but have gone on to start their own ministries. We conducted a survey recently and found

156

that one-fourth of the people at Harvest are actively involved in service in some capacity.

I have found that people who are the most enthusiastic about sharing their faith and ministering to others are often those who are youngest in the faith. Our new converts often want to immediately get involved in service. This isn't always a good idea. We require that new believers attend our church and be discipled for at least a year before they can serve. This is a way to protect them and to help them get a good spiritual foundation. Paul warned about putting new converts in such positions, where they would be targeted by the devil (1 Tim. 3:6).

Once new believers have met that requirement, we also ask them to go through some training, depending on what positions they are filling.

Six Keys to Discipling Others

Discipling others is mostly an informal matter, and it should happen naturally in the course of our life if we're walking tightly with the Lord. However, sometimes we want to be more focused in our approach. We want to "take someone on," the way Mark did with me or the way Aquila and Priscilla took on Apollos. Here are some things to keep in mind that will help in such situations:

1. EVALUATE THE PERSON'S NEED. Is this a new Christian, a person who's been a Christian a long time but who has slipped back into a sinful lifestyle, or just a struggling young person who wants someone to look up to?

2. EVALUATE THE FIT. Sometimes we're not the right person to disciple someone, and God has other options. It's almost always better, for example, to let women disciple women and men disciple men.

3. EVALUATE YOUR GIFTS. Some of us are especially good at helping others apply Scripture to real-life situations. Some of us are good encouragers. Others are gifted to help people in concrete, practical ways. We all have something to offer. Some are

gifted communicators; others are not. Discover your gifts, and give whatever you have to offer.

4. EVALUATE CHURCH RESOURCES. What Bible studies or other opportunities can you help a new believer take advantage of? Can you accompany him? Or could you call someone who's already going and try to make a connection?

5. EVALUATE YOUR COMMITMENT/ TIME FRAME. In the case of formal discipleship, sometimes it's helpful to set up a time line. "Let's get together every Tuesday for three months" can help a new believer feel more willing to sign on.

6. EVALUATE PROGRESS. How is the new believer doing? Are there signs of growth? Does this appear to be a good match? What's the next step? Are you learning from this experience as well?

> SOME OF US DISCIPLE THROUGH HOSPITALITY; OTHERS ENJOY TALKING OVER THEOLOGICAL ISSUES. DISCOVER YOUR GIFTS, AND GIVE WHATEVER YOU HAVE TO OFFER.

Jesus said in Matthew 13:12, "Whoever has, to him more will be given, and he will have abundance; but whoever does not have, even what he has will be taken away from him" (NKJV). Do you see the importance of giving out what God has given to you? Proverbs 11:25 says, "The generous soul will be made rich, and he who waters will also be watered himself" (NKJV).

As I am ministering to others, God is ministering to me. As I am giving out, I'm also taking in from God's resources. The more I give, the more God gives. You cannot out-give God. Did you know that? You have your little spoon dishing out. He has a steam shovel coming at you. God says, "I will give you more."

It's the way that God designs His wonderful truth. It is designed to be passed on. Discipleship is not a suggestion; it is a command. It is essential.

Let me close by saying this: For the sake of those who don't yet know Christ, don't forsake God's command to go and make disciples. For the sake of the young believer, don't let apathy rob you of helping him or her on the journey. For the sake of maintaining an exciting, fruit-bearing walk with God, don't ignore these commands of Jesus. There's a world full of people ripe to hear the Good News. But there are so few workers for the harvest. We need disciple makers.

May God help us be just that. Remember: It takes one to make one.

As I am ministering to others, God is ministering to me. The more I give, the more God gives.

WHO'S ACCOUNTABLE HERE?

Question: Greg, how seriously do you think a church should take discipleship when it comes to accountability, people dealing with their sins, etc? Don't a lot of people go to a big church just so they don't have to be a true disciple because no one is watching?

Answer: That can happen. Some people do attend large churches for that very reason. They can retain a certain anonymity.

I think people who are visiting for the first time resent it when someone is overbearing with them, trying to get their address or invite them to do something. People will take that next step when they are ready. We know that we have unbelievers visit our church, and we want them first and foremost to make a commitment to Christ.

However, if we found out that a person who had allegedly made a commitment to Christ was living an ungodly lifestyle (sleeping with the boyfriend or girlfriend, for instance), they would be confronted and told to stop. If they persisted, we would ask them not to attend until there had been what we call "fruits in keeping with repentance."

For people to interact and develop spiritually in a large church, they need to get involved in one of our smaller group studies (men's or women's Bible fellowship, a midweek study, home Bible study, etc.). Every person in ministry is under some person who is accountable to a ministry leader, who is accountable to one of the people on our pastoral team.

PASTOR TO PASTOR
Balance of Power

As a pastor, you are ultimately a full-time discipler. That is not only your ministry but also your occupation. Sometimes it can be frustrating, in the same way a teacher wants to wring her hands when her students don't seem to want to learn. She's giving them key insights, and they're looking out the window. You're called to disciple, but the decision to follow is out of your hands. Remember these key points, and teach them to your church:

- *Growth takes time.* You are called to instruct "with all patience."
- *This is not a performance.* Authenticity and effort need to rate as high in importance as the appearance and polish.

- *Those who lead are vulnerable to temptation.* You yourself need prayer and guidance from others.
- *Some truths are caught more than taught.* Jesus taught His disciples a lot just by being with them. He was often with the multitudes, but He made time for the twelve disciples He had chosen to be with Him. People absorb a lot by being close to the little tasks you carry out daily, the comments you make that are unprepared, and the attitude you have when you aren't in front of a crowd.
- *You can't control another's journey.* Ultimately you have to let people choose—and choose to let them learn from consequences.

TEN

UPSIDE-DOWN LOVE
The Way to Show the World

IT'S IMPOSSIBLE to study how to become an upside-down church and not talk about Jesus' second greatest command: Love your neighbor as yourself (see Matthew 19:19).

How important is it? God says it's so important that getting everything else right won't matter if we don't get this right. We can evangelize right. We can get discipleship right, teaching and learning until the sun goes down. But a church, or a person, who doesn't get love right is not getting much else right (see 1 Cor. 13).

The Bible teaches that one of the characteristic signs of the last days is that there will be more self-love than ever. Second Timothy 3:1-2 says, "Mark this: There will be terrible times in the last days. People will be lovers of themselves" (NIV).

If that doesn't describe American culture, what does? Then it goes on: "lovers of money, boastful, proud, abusive, disobedient to their parents, ungrateful, unholy, without love, unforgiving, slanderous, without self-control, brutal, not lovers of the good, treacherous, rash, conceited, lovers of pleasure rather than lovers of God." All these characteristics are but outgrowths of loving ourselves rather than loving God.

Of course, putting others first goes directly against our inclination to care about ourselves above all. But if we really want to reveal Christ to our world, our most powerful tool is love—and not just the kind of love the world is accustomed to but the kind of upside-down, outrageously forgiving, and generous love that Jesus lived out and spoke to us about.

This kind of love has as its primary concern not its own welfare but the welfare of others. This kind of love will turn the world on its ear.

But before we talk more about becoming this kind of a loving church, we need to clear up some misconceptions. First of all, what does God really mean when He says, "Love your neighbor as yourself"?

Self-Love vs. Selfless Love

This command, to love our neighbor as we love ourselves, has often been mishandled in our "me first" age. Both Christians and unbelievers have interpreted this verse to support the theory that we need to learn to love ourselves more. The logic goes like this: Before you can effectively love others, you have to first learn to love yourself. So what we really need is more self-love or "self-esteem."

But is that really what that verse is saying? That certainly would not fit the context of Scripture. Jesus is not saying we should learn to love ourselves and then, as a result, go and love our neighbor. If that's what He meant, that's exactly what He would have said. He is assuming—rightly of course!—that your first concern when you wake up in the morning is for yourself.

You may be thinking, *No, Greg, you are wrong. I hate myself.*

I understand that reaction, but why do you hate yourself so much? *Because I'm ugly. Because I'm stupid. Because I'm a loser. I just hate myself.* That may be true. But the whole point is that you want to be different because you care so much about yourself. Even in your self-loathing, you are focused on yourself. As we all are.

When you walk past a mirror or one of those storefront win-

.dows, do you ever shoot a glance at yourself? *Am I looking OK? Those pants are a little high. What's going on? I'm getting heavier.*

And how about when someone gives you a picture of you and a bunch of people—whom do you look for first? You look for yourself. You love yourself. I love myself. We need to begin there. Then we will understand what Jesus meant when He said, "Love your neighbor as yourself."

What would happen if we truly began to take Jesus at His word and lived this way? What would this do to our churches? Can you imagine what kind of world we would live in if people operated by this principle? What would it be like if we really were as concerned about others' happiness, problems, and disappointments as we are about our own?

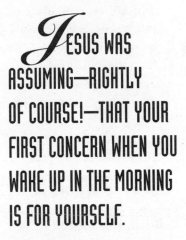

JESUS WAS ASSUMING—RIGHTLY OF COURSE!—THAT YOUR FIRST CONCERN WHEN YOU WAKE UP IN THE MORNING IS FOR YOURSELF.

No wonder the upside-down principles of love are also our greatest witness to the world; they back up everything else we are trying to do and say to unbelievers.

Remember how in Acts all the believers were as one? The response was a daily adding to their numbers. People came to Jesus because they saw how Christians loved each other.

Too often we see the opposite. I fear that we Christians are more often known for what we are against, not what we are for.

As it is, too many of us treat the world as the "enemy," and we respond to conflict or difficult people the same way the world would. Love leads people to God. Why? Because, as John says, "God is love" (see 1 John 4:8, 16). And if God is love, there can be no greater demonstration to the world of His existence than when we truly love them as God does.

PASTOR TO PASTOR

Do You Know What Your Congregation Is Reading?

B*usiness Week* magazine made this astute observation in an article on Christian retailing: "The books selling in Christian bookstores today are the touchy feely ones that focus on self-esteem, self-fulfillment, self-analysis. While devotionals, and missionary biographies gather dust on the shelves, so do books encouraging self-sacrifice."

It's embarrassing that even we believers can be obsessed with self. One popular Christian author made this statement in his book: "Christianity is an adventure of self-discovery that helps believers to become aware of their innate goodness." Innate goodness? Not according to Romans 1 and 2.

THE BIBLE WILL LEAD US TO SPIRITUAL HEALTH, BUT THROUGH THE TRUTH ABOUT OUR SINFULNESS AND THE HOPE OF FORGIVENESS AND RESTORATION.

Another book said, "The Bible makes people feel good about themselves. Many try to use it to make people hate themselves, but the Bible promotes psychological and emotional health." Is that so?

What about the statement Jesus makes to the church of Laodicea (Rev. 3:17): "You are wretched, miserable, poor, blind, and naked" (NKJV). Or James 4:8-9, which says, "Cleanse your hands, you sinners; and purify your hearts, you double-minded. Lament and mourn and weep! Let your laughter be turned to mourning and your joy to gloom" (NKJV). The Bible will lead us to spiritual health, but it will do so through the truth about our sinfulness and the hope of forgiveness and restoration. It's not just a feel-good-about-yourself book. Most of the time, Jesus (and all the prophets, Old Testament and New) are trying to get people to wake up to what *isn't* good—so that healing can begin.

I'm not against self-esteem, and I'm certainly not against emotional healing. But we need to be careful not to misuse Scripture to support these quests as ends in themselves. And we also need to make sure we're going to God, to His Word, for help.

HATE VS. HUMILITY

Question: Greg, are you saying that the Bible teaches us to hate ourselves? And how come humility gets no respect these days?

Answer: Let's understand. The Bible does *not* teach self-hate. The Bible does not teach that I am to be some miserable, always-down-on-myself person. The Bible is saying that you should see yourself as you are. You love yourself. But God is asking that instead of being so concerned about yourself, you give that same energy to others. That's part of what it means to deny yourself.

The Bible's main purpose is not to promote psychological encouragement or emotional health (although these are natural results of a thriving relationship with God). The Bible is given to reveal who God is. It is here to tell us how to come in contact with Him and how to be like Him. That is going to require that we see ourselves as we really are: Sinners separated from a God whom we have offended by our willful disobedience and the breaking of His commandments.

God's Upside-Down Love

It has been said that "Christians are living epistles; written by God and read by men." You are the only Bible some people are ever going to read. Upon hearing that you are a Christian, they will carefully watch your every move. They will want to see if your faith is real.

We may protest and say, "Well, no one is perfect, and people shouldn't expect too much of me!" That may be true, but like it or not, people are basing their opinion about God on you. We as a church are here to represent Jesus Christ to this world.

Most of us don't have a problem loving those who love us or giving to those who can give something back. We easily love our Christian friend who likes the same books and music we do. But Jesus said, "If you love those who love you, what reward will you get? Are not even the tax collectors doing that? And if you greet only your brothers, what are you doing more than others? Do not even pagans do that? Be perfect, therefore, as your heavenly Father is perfect" (Matt. 5:46-48, NIV).

Jesus is saying, in essence, "If you love those who love you and hang out with your friends and treat them well . . . so what? What does that prove? Even non-Christians love people who love them. I'm asking you to be different."

Just as Jesus has given us radical principles of discipleship, He repeatedly asks us to go one step farther. Consider these upside-down commands about relationships found in the Sermon on the Mount (Matt. 5–7).

- *Love your enemies and pray for those who persecute you.* Our tendency is to hate our "enemy"—that guy at the office who keeps trying to take credit for everything and make us look incompetent.
- *If someone strikes your right cheek, turn to him the other also.* Our tendency is to slap back—cut off the guy on the freeway who cut us off.

- *If someone forces you to go one mile, go with him two miles.* Our tendency is to make sure no one takes advantage of us.
- *Freely forgive those who don't deserve it—over and over again.* Our tendency is to wait for—or demand—an apology before we even consider forgiveness.
- *Judge yourself first—and more harshly than others.* Our tendency is to be hypercritical of others and to be slow to see our own errors.

We live in a culture that tells us to forget about others. Think only of yourself. Other people are out for themselves, and if you lower your guard, they will rip you off. They will take advantage of you. Your main job in life is to look out for number one.

We think, *What about me? What about my needs?* What if we adjusted our thinking to *Forget about me. What about that person over there?*

And if someone hurts you, we think it's OK if you hurt them back,

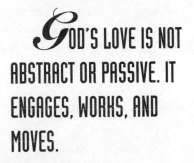

God's Love is not abstract or passive. It engages, works, and moves.

get your pound of flesh. We exalt vengeance as a virtue, and we scoff at the person who forgives or turns the other cheek. If someone offends you, sue them. That's the operative phrase of the day.

Jesus is saying here that we have to do a flip-flop. We can't let this world squeeze us into its mold.

None of this comes naturally. But that's just the point, and that's the reason this love is powerful. Love isn't a feeling; love is fully love only when it acts. God's love is not abstract or passive. It is active. It engages, works, and moves. And that's good news, because it means that we can learn to love. We can grow in love. We can learn to love God's way.

God's Love Lessons

When one wants to get a clear picture of how this love Jesus commands us to have is supposed to look, 1 Corinthians 13 is a great place to start. It is perhaps the most definitive chapter on love in the Bible, and it goes straight to the heart of our struggles to love in the most daily and intimate settings.

But this section about love is useful to us because it does not focus so much on what love is. Rather, it focuses on what love does and does not do. The purpose of Paul's little prism here in 1 Corinthians 13 is not to give a technical analysis of love but to break it into understandable pieces so that we can more easily apply it in practical ways. If you really want to feel uncomfortable, go to 1 Corinthians 13, take out the word *love*, and put your name in its place. That can be discouraging. But there's another name you can insert in there that fits very well: Jesus. And as we read these verses, you will see that this passage is a true portrait of who Jesus is.

> *Love suffers long and is kind; love does not envy; love does not parade itself, is not puffed up; does not behave rudely, does not seek its own, is not provoked, thinks no evil; does not rejoice in iniquity, but rejoices in the truth; bears all things, believes all things, hopes all things, endures all things.* 1 Cor. 13:4-7, NKJV

The first thing we are told is that love is patient. Another way to translate that phrase is to say that love is long tempered. The word used here is common in the New Testament and is used almost exclusively with reference to being patient with people rather than being patient with circumstances or events. Love is willing to be inconvenienced or taken advantage of by a person over and over again.

Stephen's last words as he had his young life taken from him are a good example of patient love. As he was being stoned to death, he said, "Lord, do not hold this sin against them" (Acts

7:60, NIV). This is the same kind of love Jesus spoke of that turns the other cheek. This kind of love has as its primary concern not its own welfare but the welfare of others.

God's love is patient. It is long tempered.

Perhaps there is a person you work with or maybe a member of your family. This person may not be a Christian and seems to always be giving you a hard time. He makes jokes at your expense, quickly reminds you when you are not practicing what you preach, bombards you with difficult questions, and so on. You have thought about letting him really have it; you know, just giving him a piece of your mind. God knows he deserves it.

But instead, you just keep loving him. You try your best to answer his questions. You thank him when he points out that you are not living as you ought. Don't you realize how powerful that attitude and behavior are when coupled with the message you proclaim? It's a practically irresistible combination!

Remember Stephen. I believe it was his love that penetrated the hardened shell around the heart of Saul of Tarsus. Saul was holding the robes of the people who were stoning Stephen. He must have heard Stephen praying that God would forgive all of them.

The next attribute mentioned is kindness. To be kind means to be useful, serving, gracious. It is active goodwill. It does not merely desire the welfare of others; Philippians 2:3-4 says, "Let nothing be done through selfish ambition or conceit, but in lowliness of mind let each esteem others better than himself. Let each of you look out not only for his own interests, but also for the interests of others" (NKJV).

Love is active. If you wait for this emotion to come, you may never experience kindness. You may say to yourself, "I just don't feel kind; therefore it would be hypocritical of me to help that person. I don't feel the emotion, so it wouldn't be sincere if I were to reach out to her."

Just be kind, even if you don't feel kind. That's what God's love is.

Paul goes on to give us eight descriptions of what love is *not,* beginning with envious and jealous.

There are two kinds of jealousy. One says, "I want what someone else has." If they have a better car, house, job, even wife or husband, we secretly, and maybe not so secretly, wish we had the same. Isn't it amazing how you can be completely content with what you have until you see someone who has more of something or simply something different?

When I was a little boy, I had gotten a great haul one Christmas—lots of toys. I was so happy—until I went over to my friend's house. He had gotten a toy I'd never seen before. It was a little plastic scuba diver. You put batteries in him, and his little flippers kicked in the water. I thought that was the coolest toy ever made, and suddenly all of my toys were meaningless. I figured that my mom didn't really care about me. I actually went home and said, "Why didn't you get me this toy?"

Why did I feel that way? I was jealous. I wanted what he had.

Just accept the fact that there are always going to be people better off than you are. No matter how high you climb your ladder, how handsome or beautiful you are, or how successful in your field, someone is going to walk right over you. They are going to go past you. *How come they can do that?* Jealousy possesses us.

The second kind of jealousy is more subtle. I don't want what someone has. I wish *that person* didn't have what he or she has. I am so jealous of what they have that I would rather it be taken away from them. That's more than selfishness. It's actually desiring evil for someone else.

A familiar story in the Old Testament illustrates this kind of jealousy well. There were two mothers who both had babies, and they were all asleep in the same room. One night one of the mothers rolled over on her newborn and suffocated it, and it died. So she took the live baby from the other sleeping mother and put it in her bed and replaced it with her own dead baby.

When they woke up the next morning, the other mother saw immediately that this dead baby was not hers. "This is your baby. Why did you do this?" she asks the other woman.

"That's your baby. I can't help it if it died," she answers.

"You took my baby."

"No. It's my baby."

So they went to see King Solomon, who was renowned for his God-given wisdom. Both mothers were claiming to be the baby's mother. Solomon asked for wisdom from the Lord. Then he said, "I have the answer. Let's cut the baby in half. You can have one half. You can have the other."

The real mother said, "No. Just give the baby to her. She can have it."

The other woman said, "I like the idea. Cut the baby in half."

Then Solomon said, "I know who the real mother is. Give it to this woman, the one who wanted the child to live."

Jealousy in its extreme is willing to see all kinds of people suffer. James 3:14-16 says, "If you are bitterly jealous and there is selfish ambition in your hearts, don't brag about being wise. That is the worst kind of lie. . . . For wherever there is jealousy and selfish ambition, there you will find disorder and every kind of evil" (NLT).

TRUE LOVE HAS GOOD MANNERS. THAT'S SOMETHING THAT IS LARGELY LOST TODAY. WE SAY, "IF MY BEHAVIOR OFFENDS SOMEONE ELSE, THAT'S THEIR PROBLEM."

God's love is not jealous. And as we read on, it "does not parade itself."

Some people want everybody else to know how much they paid for a certain item or how high their IQ is or even how spiritual they think they are. They may brag about how much time they spend in prayer or how many people they have personally led to the Lord. They may go on and on about their church—its programs and big budget. God's kind of love does not brag.

Bragging is the other side of jealousy. Jealousy is wanting what someone else has. Bragging is trying to make others jealous of what we have.

In verse 5 of 1 Corinthians we're told that love does not behave rudely. True love has good manners. That's something that is largely lost today. We say, "If my behavior offends someone else, that's their problem. They have to get over it." But you are part of the body of Christ, and you should consider what other people are experiencing.

In this day of "road rage" and downright rudeness practically everywhere, a bit of kindness and some good manners can go a long way.

Verse 5 tells us that God's love is not provoked. It is not aroused to anger. It thinks no evil, which means it doesn't keep a record of the wrongs that are done to it. Unlike a common human response:

Someone wrongs you, and you say, "I can't believe you did that again."

"Again? When did I do it?"

"Fourteen years ago. Actually, fourteen years, three months, two weeks, ten hours, twenty-eight minutes, and four seconds."

"Are you crazy?"

"I keep records. Because I don't get mad; I get even."

That's not God's love.

Someone took advantage of you. Forget about it. They do it again. Forget about it. Don't worry about it. Just let it go. It doesn't matter. That's how God's love is.

Listen to this: Love "believes all things." Another way to translate this statement in verse 7 is to say that love believes all *good* things or love believes the best. It means that as a member of the body of Christ, a Christian who is loving, you are not always suspicious of others. You are not a cynic. If a fellow member of the church is accused of something wrong, you will consider him or her innocent until proven guilty. Not only that, you will stick up for that person.

But how often someone will come and say, "Did you hear about so-and-so?"

"No. What?"

"He has been accused of this and that."

"I always knew it." How often we will believe a rumor.

Rather, you should say, "Stop right there. Have you gone to so-and-so and talked about it?"

"No. I can't go to him. He would deny it."

"Maybe he didn't do it. Let's go to him right now. Because I don't believe he would do such a thing."

You should stick up for that person. But, no, in these days so often we will believe the worst. And then we will even add to it.

But then how sad it is and how embarrassing it is when we find out this was a complete fabrication and we actually fanned the flame of the gossip/slander fire by believing it and even spreading it to others. How hard it is when something unkind or untrue is said about us and we find that people believe it without even asking us. That's not the way we should be. God's love believes the best of every person.

Finally, verse 7 says that love *endures* all things. It refuses to give up. It refuses to surrender, to stop believing or hoping. Love will simply not stop loving.

You may be thinking, *Now, Greg, please. How could we ever live up to these standards? It's impossible.*

Yes, it is. By human effort it's impossible. But this is what we should be aiming toward. The Bible says God's love is shed abroad in our heart by the Holy Spirit. We need to cooperate with that by saying, "Lord, I am not this way. I am not always thinking the best of every person. I am not always mannerly, kind, or long tempered. Lord, I acknowledge my weakness, and I want to change."

The Bible tells us that the fruit of the Spirit is love. And this fruit will come as a result of abiding in Christ, of seeking to be more like Him each and every day.

PASTOR TO PASTOR
Five Ways to Love the World

James tells us that people will know we have faith by our works (see James 2:14-24). Faith justifies us before God. Works justify us before people. This world is desperate to see tangible demonstrations of the church loving, not condemning.

Here are some practical ideas (ones that we have practiced at our church).

1. Run a home for unwed mothers.
People know that we Christians are against abortion. Instead of waving placards down at the local abortion clinic, how about establishing a home for unwed mothers? We should provide a place where these mothers-to-be can be encouraged and given the means to carry their pregnancies to term, whether that means helping them make motherhood work for themselves or finding adoptive parents for the baby.

In addition to a home, our church also has a hotline for pregnant women; it's called Heartline. They call, maybe thinking we will refer them to the local abortion clinic. Instead, we encourage them to carry their pregnancy to term.

2. Minister to people in convalescent homes.
So many of our elderly people have been forgotten and, in some cases, completely abandoned by their family and friends. A little love on the part of a Christian there can go a long way.

We send people from our church over at Christmastime to sing Christmas carols for them. But all through the year, teams of people from our congregation go and read to them, sing to them, just be there. Many have come to know Christ as a result.

3. Feed hungry people.

We go out on Saturdays into the local parks and set up a little kitchen and feed people.

We have our worship group get up and sing some songs; then someone shares a gospel message; then we feed them a great meal.

During Christmas we also distribute special baskets filled with food for a Christmas dinner (with all the trimmings!), along with gospel tracts.

4. Distribute clothing.

Our church has a ministry called The Lord's Closet.

We ask people from our congregation to give us their unwanted clothing. We store it and give it to people who are in need. We also take clothing to the parks when we're feeding people and distribute it there.

5. Visit prisoners.

Visiting prisoners who, like the elderly, have been forgotten by family and friends, can really make a difference in their life.

We have teams that go into our prisons and juvenile halls and share the gospel with the inmates, and the result has been many of them coming to know Jesus Christ.

One in Spirit

Until now we've been talking about how to express love in relationships and to the world in general. But what about love in the church—locally and at large? The world needs to know God's love. We must remember that the world is watching. And ultimately it is our love for each other in the church that is one of our greatest illustrations of who Christ is.

We, the church, are God's representatives on earth. And if we present to the world a church that is full of dissension, how can we effectively present Christ? He said that a building divided against itself cannot stand. And yet the church today is so often a setting for squabbles and dissension. We behave just like the world, only we do it in a beautiful building and attach spiritual terms to our ugly behavior.

Remember the love and unity of the early church described in Acts 2? That is our example. The original language used to describe this kind of love, here and other places in the Word, is the Greek word *koinonia*. We have many translations of this word into the English language, the most common being the word *fellowship*. But it can also be translated into the words *communion, distribution, contribution, partnership, partakership*. It describes a kind of love that is based on joint effort and purpose.

You know, some Christians actually have a hard time with Christians. It's easier to love people in the world because they don't know any better. They're supposed to be sinners. But those in the family of Christ . . . sometimes it's hardest to love those nearest to us in the pew. We expect more of them and from them (and they of us). And too often the result is bitterness and dissension.

The upside-down church is a church that is committed to loving at all costs. It is ready to make peace, to promote harmony, to lay aside pride and differences. A lot of churches are looking around for the right growth plan or the right inner framework. And that's great. God's church needs administration and organization. But what if we really worked on love?

When the world peeks in the windows of your church, what does it see? Does it see a bunch of people who really love each other? Does it see unity? fellowship? Or does the world look in your church and see just another organization or institution where people compete and strive and argue? Do they see us competing to serve or struggling for positions of power? Jesus said "By this all will know that you are My disciples, if you have love for one another" (John 13:35, NKJV).

It was this very thing that origi-nally got my attention as an un-believer. It was 1970. The sixties were over, but the ideas of love and brotherhood were still being talked about. There was still the belief that we, the younger genera-tion, would not go the way of the Establishment. We would cast aside labels and prejudice and really love each other as brothers and sisters in the human family.

THE UPSIDE-DOWN CHURCH IS READY TO MAKE PEACE, TO PROMOTE HARMONY, TO LAY ASIDE PRIDE AND DIFFERENCES.

A sweet sentiment—it just didn't work. I quickly realized that we were chasing after a mirage. I still loved the idea; I just felt it was basically unattainable. Then I began to notice this group of very committed Christians on my high school campus. We very unaffectionately referred to them as the "Jesus freaks."

They seemed to really be experiencing what others only talked about. They called each other brother and sister but somehow seemed to mean it. After a class was over, I would see them hugging each other and saying strange things like, "I'll be praying for you!"

Having always been quite skeptical, I had a hard time believ-ing this was not all some kind of act. So I started watching the Christians very carefully. They were starting to bug me a little bit, because if they were right, then that meant I was wrong. If God could actually be known and they had a relationship with

Him, that meant that I did not. So I watched them day in and day out, just waiting for one of them to slip up or break ranks and announce, "This has all been a big act."

But that never happened—for one simple reason. It was real. They actually did love one another. It was that fact that initially got me looking into the claims of Christ.

How would you, and how would your church, hold up under such scrutiny?

ELEVEN

KNOCK, KNOCK, WHO'S PRAYING?
The Power of
Upside-Down Prayer

SOMETIMES the Bible reminds me of the number one rule of fiction writing. It goes something like this: Get your character into a terribly hopeless, perilous position, a real dilemma with no way out. And then, just when things can't get any worse for your hero—make them much, much worse.

Of course, in the Bible this is usually where God steps in. And unlike a fiction story, God's stories are intended to do more than keep us on the edge of our seat. He wants us to understand how His kingdom principles work. And so He doesn't just say, "Pray." He *shows* through the lives of others what happens when people pray—and when they don't.

In Acts 12, starting in verse 1, we read a great story about how God redeemed a desperate situation through the power of prayer.

First, let's meet the bad guy—Herod. This name, *Herod,* appears quite often in the New Testament because there were actually a number of Herods, all related. The first Herod we read about was Herod the Great. He was king during the time of the birth of Christ. He had a son named Herod Antipas, who was eventually responsible for the beheading of John the Baptist. This Herod also had a son named Herod (Did anyone suggest

"Frank" or "Sam"?). This is Herod Agrippa, and he's the Herod we read about in Acts.

> *Now about that time Herod the king stretched out his hand to harass some from the church. Then he killed James the brother of John with the sword. And because he saw that it pleased the Jews, he proceeded further to seize Peter also.* Acts 12:1-3, NKJV

Immediately we learn that Herod Agrippa was a typical politician in the most negative sense. He wasn't interested in serving the people he represented but in being popular and powerful among them. Whatever made them happy, he'd do. Today he'd be one of those scandal-plagued politicians who shapes his policies around opinion polls and knows how to make use of a pandering media.

We read on:

> *Now it was during the Days of Unleavened Bread. So when he had arrested him, he put him in prison, and delivered him to four squads of soldiers to keep him, intending to bring him before the people after Passover.* Acts 12:3-4, NKJV

Herod had a reason for stationing so many soldiers around Peter in jail. He didn't want another resurrection episode—or another escape attempt. In the forefront of his mind was the tomb fiasco—the men guarding Jesus' tomb had fallen asleep. He was probably thinking also about the last time Peter was in prison. Just when Herod was sure Peter was under lock and key, he'd escaped.

Picture it. Someone said, "Hey, Peter is out there in the streets preaching."

"No," replied Herod with confidence, "Peter's in prison. Put him there myself."

"Oh, really? So then why is he out there preaching Christ?"

"What?!"

Peter must have seemed to Herod like James Bond does to his enemies in the movies. So it's not surprising that this time Herod took every precaution against Peter's escape—short of sitting on top of Peter himself.

Now let's consider Peter's position for a moment. He's the good guy in this story, and he's not just in prison; he's behind two locked gates, chained to two guards, and guarded by fourteen more. His fellow apostle James has been killed, and the situation for the church, as well as for Peter, has gone from grim to seemingly hopeless.

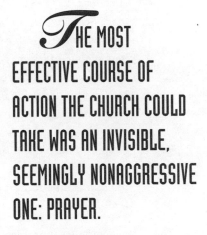

THE MOST EFFECTIVE COURSE OF ACTION THE CHURCH COULD TAKE WAS AN INVISIBLE, SEEMINGLY NONAGGRESSIVE ONE: PRAYER.

So what does the church do? We read on: "Peter was therefore kept in prison, but constant prayer was offered to God for him by the church" (Acts 12:5, NKJV).

Notice that we don't read "The church boycotted all products made by Rome" or "The church had a sit-in in Herod's court." They didn't write to their local representative down there at the Roman Senate to do something about this immediately.

Some of the political options I mentioned do have their place. But the church at large must remember that these actions aren't the solution. They're human methods, and they are attempts to change people. *The most effective course of action the church could take was an invisible, seemingly nonaggressive one: prayer.*

We pick up the story again in verse 6.

> *And when Herod was about to bring him out, that night Peter was sleeping, bound with two chains between two soldiers; and the guards before the door were keeping the*

prison. Now behold, an angel of the Lord stood by him, and a light shone in the prison; and he struck Peter on the side and raised him up, saying, "Arise quickly!" And his chains fell off his hands. Then the angel said to him, "Gird yourself and tie on your sandals"; and so he did. And he said to him, "Put on your garment and follow me." So he went out and followed him, and did not know that what was done by the angel was real, but thought he was seeing a vision. When they were past the first and the second guard posts, they came to the iron gate that leads to the city, which opened to them of its own accord; and they went out and went down one street, and immediately the angel departed from him. And when Peter had come to himself, he said, "Now I know for certain that the Lord has sent His angel, and has delivered me from the hand of Herod and from all the expectation of the Jewish people." Acts 12:6-11, NKJV

There is power in prayer, and Peter knew it. The early church knew it. Though all of the doors were closed, one remained open: the door of prayer. This was and is the church's secret weapon and its source of power.

A Question of Faith

If this story stopped there, it would make the point that prayer works. However, if you read on, you'll notice that the disciples didn't do *everything* right. They prayed, yes. They prayed continually—earnestly, in unity. But they also doubted.

So, when he had considered this, he came to the house of Mary, the mother of John whose surname was Mark, where many were gathered together praying. And as Peter knocked at the door of the gate, a girl named Rhoda came to answer. When she recognized Peter's voice, because of her gladness she did not open the gate, but ran in and announced that Peter stood before the gate. But they said to her, "You are beside yourself!" Yet she kept insisting that it was so. So they said, "It is his angel." Now Peter continued knocking; and when they opened the door and saw him, they were astonished. Acts 12:12-16, NKJV

Picture this scene. Peter runs over to the house. He knocks on the door. Inside, the gathered church is praying. "Oh, Lord," they may have pleaded, "this is the last night before our beloved Peter is to be executed, as James was. Dear God, please deliver our—"

A knock sounds, but they keep praying, "Deliver our brother, and somehow get him out safely—"

There's the knock on the door again. Finally Rhoda gets up to answer it. She reappears moments later and interrupts. "Excuse me—"

"Lord, this is Peter, the Peter that you love. We pray—"

"Excuse me."

"What is it?"

"Peter is at the door."

"Are you crazy?"

Notice now the plural pronouns. "They" opened the door and "they" were astonished. It seems that for safety's sake the believers decided to open the door cautiously and face together what was on the other side. They are peering out . . .

And there's Peter, smiling. "Hi, everybody. God answered your prayers. Here I am."

I am so glad this is in the Bible. Not just because it's comical but because it reminds all of us that the apostles and leaders of the early church were people just like us.

But let's not miss the spiritual point. Not only does God answer prayer, but His power is not dependent on our praying perfectly. This passage, among others, debunks the popular teaching among some that says our faith makes all the difference in prayer and that faith is some kind of active force that we have to harness and use. We are told that we have to say the right thing. We have to give a "positive confession." We have to speak the miracle into existence. According to this theology, almost everything about prayer revolves around the quality of our faith.

Not ONLY DOES GOD ANSWER PRAYER, BUT HIS POWER IS NOT DEPENDENT ON OUR PRAYING PERFECTLY.

It certainly was a good thing for Peter that this isn't true! Faith has a crucial place in prayer, but we should never say or think, "I want to pray for this, but I don't think I have enough faith." Instead, we should pray anyway, saying, "Lord, I believe; help my unbelief."

We must remember that there are certain things only God can do. We must do what only *we* can do. Only I can repent of my sin. Only I can believe the promises of God. Only I can discipline myself.

But only God can convert people. Only God can create a soul. Only God can forgive sin and take our guilt away. I have got to do my part, and God will do His part. My part is to pray in obedience and with as much faith as I can muster. God's part is to answer prayer.

An Upside-Down Approach to Prayer

How easy it is for us to approach prayer—our communication with God—from a human perspective. We begin to think of prayer as if it were a Coke machine. Insert the requests, and wait for the answers to come out. Or we may begin to think of prayer as a way to get God to conform to our wishes rather than help us conform to His.

Prayer in itself is a completely spiritual act. And effective prayer operates on God's upside-down kingdom principles. God

186

describes these principles for us clearly in His word. Again and again He tells how we should pray, what we should pray for, and when we should pray.

1. Pray as the first resort—not the last.
When the believers learned that Peter was in prison, they said, "All right, we need a big gun here. We have trouble. What are we going to do? Let's pray."

Unfortunately, this is usually not our first inclination. We pray after we've exhausted all our own means of rescue. We pray when it becomes clear that we are completely helpless. For example, let's say you don't have enough money to pay your bills. If you're like most of us, first you might borrow the money from a credit card. If it's maxed out, you might call a friend to borrow some money. If that fails, you might go so far as to call a relative. And then finally, perhaps after trying strangers from the phone book, you reluctantly pray. At this point, what have you got to lose?

But what you should be asking yourself is, *What have I lost by not praying?*

The Bible says, "You do not have, because you do not ask God"

I HAVE PRAYED FOR SOME REALLY STUPID THINGS. AND I AM SO GLAD THE LORD OVERRULED AND SAID, "OH, GREG, FORGET IT. I'M NOT GOING TO DO THAT TO YOU."

(James 4:2, NIV). It is my firm conviction that many Christians don't have God's provision, healing, and blessing in their lives simply because they have not asked for it.

I don't believe that God heals everyone or will give you everything you might ask for. But many of us are missing out on many of the things God has for us simply because we don't ask. Prayer should not be a last resort. It should be the first thing we do.

2. Pray for what God wants—not what you want.
Our natural impulse is to pray for what we want, but upside-down prayer is in line with what *God* wants. Prayer that is powerful is offered according to God's will. First John 5:14-15 says, "This is the confidence that we have in Him, that if we ask anything according to His will, He hears us. And . . . we have the petitions that we have asked of Him" (NKJV).

This is reassuring because it means that nothing lies outside of the reach of prayer except what lies outside of the will of God. And we should be grateful. I have prayed for some really stupid things in my life. And I am so glad the Lord overruled and said, "Oh, Greg, forget it. I'm not going to do that to you. I love you too much."

So what we want to do is get into an alignment with the will of God. How do you learn about God's will, about His purpose, His character and mind, His heart, and His plan? Through the pages of Scripture and through spending time talking to Him.

There's really no point in praying for God to give you something if Scripture states that what you want is immoral or clearly outside of God's will. For instance, let's say that two people are in an immoral relationship. They don't need to bother praying that God will bless this union, because the Bible clearly says, "Thou shall not commit adultery."

But there are certain things God tells us we can *always* pray for—because they are always His will. For example, He tells us we can pray for wisdom. James says, "If any of you lacks wisdom, he should ask God, who gives generously to all without finding fault, and it will be given to him" (James 1:5, NIV).

We can always pray for His provision. Philippians 4:19 says, "My God will meet all your needs according to his glorious riches in Christ Jesus" (NIV). This verse doesn't say that God will provide for our "greeds." If He turns down a request, we don't need that thing the way we think we do.

188

We can always pray for protection. Psalm 91:5-7 says, "Do not be afraid of the terrors of the night, nor fear the dangers of the day, nor dread the plague that stalks in darkness, nor the disaster that strikes at midday. Though a thousand fall at your side, though ten thousand are dying around you, these evils will not touch you" (NLT).

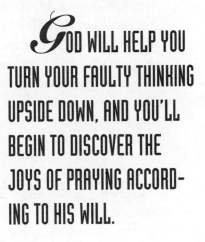

Prayer is not our permission to order God around. He is not "our bellhop who art in heaven." Prayer is not moving God your way; it is moving yourself His way. And that is the amazing thing about prayer. When you spend time in prayer, God will help you turn your faulty thinking upside down, and you'll begin to discover the joys of praying according to His will.

3. Pray earnestly—even when you don't feel like it.
Remember what we read in Acts 12:5: "Constant prayer was offered to God for him by the church" (NKJV).

The word *constant* not only speaks of a regular, continuous prayer but in the original language can be translated "earnestly" or even "with agony." It is a word that implies a soul's stretching out or reaching forward to accomplish or touch something.

Our natural impulse is to be lazy. We might pray, "Lord, would you do this? Thank you. Amen." Or "Lord, save the world. Amen." But the right approach to prayer is specific, focused, and heartfelt. "Lord, I am bringing this person before you today. Lord, I pray you will save her soul. I pray that you will bring her to a realization of her own need for you. Lord, I pray you will send Christians who speak the truth to cross her path today. . . ."

4. Pray with persistence.

This point is related to the last one. How easy it is for us to ask with passion—but then give up quickly when we don't see change immediately. God answers prayer on His timetable, not on ours. And He has told us that it's OK to ask more than once. In fact, in the parable of the widow knocking on the judge's door, Jesus was commanding us to be persistent. And Jesus said, "Man ought always to pray and never give up" (Luke 18:1, paraphrased).

Notice that Peter was not released until the very night before his planned execution. The Lord delayed His answer. The Christians were praying, and nothing was happening. They kept praying, and Peter was still in prison. But they kept praying still. And when the time was right, God answered.

Perhaps you have been praying for a loved one's salvation for a long time, maybe for months or even years. Keep praying—if it takes thirty years. Don't do the ordinary thing and give up or give in. That kind of prayer will never change the world. But persistent, passionate prayer will avail much in God's time. And that's a promise.

5. Pray with others—not just by and for yourself.

Often our impulse is to mind our own business when it comes to prayer, but upside-down prayer seeks others who share our burden—and shares theirs as well.

"Constant prayer was offered to God for [Peter] by the church." There is power in united prayer. It's important that the church pray together—in regular worship services and outside regular services. Church people need to pray for each other and for the world.

When we hold our crusades, we encourage people to pray together for unbelievers. We pass out a card and ask each person to write down the names of five people they know who are not Christians. Then they will gather in groups of three or four and pray for these people.

Why is that important? Because Jesus said, "If two of you agree on earth concerning anything that they ask, it will be done for them by My Father in heaven" (Matt. 18:19, NKJV).

Jesus is not simply emphasizing the idea of two people in agreement *in general.* He is implying that these are two people with the same God-given burden who are sure of His will, in agreement with the Spirit of God and with one another.

With whom are you praying? Are you taking advantage of joint prayers? Sometimes we can have faith for something that someone else does not have faith for. And when we extend our prayers beyond our own private agenda, we put ourselves in a position to be used by God. Praying with someone is not a small thing. It is one of the greatest things you have to offer a brother or sister in the Lord.

6. Pray with faith in God—regardless of His answer.
So often we confuse the prayer of faith—the prayer that trusts in God—with the prayer of confidence in a specific outcome. And when God's answer does not match ours, we wonder if we didn't have enough faith. We wonder if God even heard our prayer. I prayed for a job at Microsoft, and I didn't get it. How much better to put our faith in God, not in what we think His answers should be.

ARE YOU TAKING ADVANTAGE OF JOINT PRAYERS? SOMETIMES WE CAN HAVE FAITH FOR SOMETHING THAT SOMEONE ELSE DOESN'T HAVE FAITH FOR.

In the story we read, Peter seemed to have this kind of faith. How do we know? Verse 6 says that Peter was sleeping. That's amazing in itself. Would you be able to sleep if you knew you were going to be put to death the next morning? Peter was probably the only Christian in Jerusalem asleep that night. Everyone else was praying for him. Then Peter thought he was having a vision when the angel led him out of prison. We might think that if Peter had had real faith, he would have known that it wasn't a vision, that he was really being rescued.

> *W*HEN WE EXTEND OUR PRAYERS BEYOND OUR OWN AGENDA, WE PUT OURSELVES IN A POSITION TO BE USED BY GOD.

Peter's faith was in God, not in a specific answer to prayer. Keep in mind that the church must have also prayed for James as well as for Peter. Yet James was killed. And Peter knew this. His faith in God would not have been misplaced—even if he had been executed that night. Peter had faith that God heard his and the church's prayers. But he could sleep because his faith was big enough to trust God's will—*even if he wasn't rescued.*

True faith in prayer hinges on our trust in God, in His goodness and His rightness. It doesn't hinge on how much confidence we can muster that God is going to answer a specific prayer a certain way.

Miracles Knocking

Maybe you are in a situation right now and you're saying, "It is hopeless. I don't know what to do."

Pray.

"But I just—"

Pray. Let your prayer be unto God. Get your Christian friends to pray with you. Pray with fervor and with energy. Pray continually. Don't give up. You just don't know what the Lord is going to do.

At the beginning of this story we see a seemingly all-powerful Herod wreaking havoc on the church. Herod had on his side the power of the sword and the threat of prison. What did the church have? They had prayer. And they used it.

The story ends with Herod's giving a great speech that was met with the adulation of the people chanting, "The voice of a god and not of a man!" The Jewish historian Josephus adds the detail that when Herod gave this speech, he was dressed in a tunic that was made completely of silver and shone so brightly that the people hailed him as a god.

Picture this. Here was Herod in his silver frock. The sun was reflecting off him. The people were chanting in unison, "The voice of a god and not of a man!"

And then God's judgment came upon him, and he died. That is how the chapter ends.

Look at how things change. The chapter opened with James dead, Peter in prison, and Herod in triumph. It closed with Herod dead, Peter free, and the Word of God in triumph. In the end God will always have His way. It ain't over till it's over.

The kind of prayer that took place in the early church is the kind of prayer we need today. A miracle might be outside the very same door God seems to have shut. Prayer is how we open the door to receive it.

TRUE FAITH IN PRAYER DOESN'T HINGE ON HOW MUCH CONFIDENCE WE CAN MUSTER THAT GOD IS GOING TO ANSWER A SPECIFIC PRAYER A CERTAIN WAY.

Maybe you're a pastor whose church is having conflict. Or maybe your attendance has dropped off. Have you prayed? Have you prayed with faith in God?

Today, God wants to do the same things in our world and in your life that He was doing in Peter's day. Be careful. Is there a miracle knocking?

THE LORD'S PRAYER

Question: How do you recommend that a church prioritize prayer?

Answer: In addition to our many prayer meetings through the week, we have done a special intercessory prayer meeting on Sunday morning.

We modeled it after the Lord's Prayer. The prayer Jesus taught us, which really is a model for all prayer, breaks into two sections. The first three statements ("Our Father who art in heaven, hallowed be Your name, Your kingdom come, Your will be done") deal with God's glory. The second ("Give us this day our daily bread, forgive us our debts, lead not into temptation") deal with our need.

So we would start with teaching segment number one. This would introduce the prayer, and the teacher (I would have three of our associate pastors teach this) would teach on coming before God with reverence and thanksgiving and ask for His will and kingdom in our life. Then there would be a musical break that would emphasize in song these themes, and individual people we had already picked from our congregation, who would be sitting on the platform, would come and pray relatively short prayers along those lines.

Then we would go to the next sections and include intercessory prayer for our leaders, nation, church, etc. There would be prayer for those in special need and so forth. It's a way to model prayer and at the same time drop it right in the lap of someone on Sunday morning who would not necessarily attend one of our other prayer meetings.

TWELVE

MORE THAN MUSIC

How to Worship in
Spirit and Truth

A FEW YEARS ago I was given an opportunity to go to a Paul McCartney concert at the Anaheim Stadium. I've liked many of his songs, especially ones he recorded with the Beatles. We have held our crusades at the same venue over the years, so I was intrigued by the idea of seeing a different event there. And the price was right; the seats were given to me free of charge.

As it turned out, a lot that went on felt very familiar. For example, Paul McCartney got on stage and went through his litany of Beatles songs, wildly shaking his hair as if he were still twenty.

But something happened toward the end of the concert that caught me a little off guard. As the strains of a well-known Beatle anthem began, suddenly the stage was lit up with a stained-glass motif, making it look quite a bit like a cathedral. And then thousands and thousands of Bic lighters lit the stadium, and everyone began to sway and sing along to the words of "Let It Be."

I didn't have a Bic lighter to hold up. But as I looked around at that scene, I thought, "This is about as close as this world gets to having a worship experience. The lights. The sense of unity. The voices lifted with affection and even a kind of reverence."

And then I was struck with how much more we Christians have in our worship experience. Think about it. We have a light much greater than a flimsy Bic. We have a Savior so much greater than any rock star. And when we gather together to sing, we really don't want to just "let it be." We want to change the world.

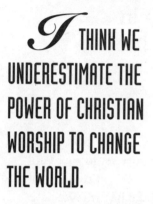

I THINK WE UNDERESTIMATE THE POWER OF CHRISTIAN WORSHIP TO CHANGE THE WORLD.

I think we underestimate the power of Christian worship to do just that—to change the world. For some reason, we stand in awe of the pop culture's power to influence kids through music. But the church is trying so hard to relate to a secular culture that too often we forget that this culture is an arena where our strengths lie as well. We forget that worship can be a powerful tool for evangelism.

Psalm 40:3 declares, "He has given me a new song to sing, a hymn of praise to our God. Many will see what he has done and be astounded. They will put their trust in the Lord" (NLT).

If we're going to turn the world upside down, we're not going to do it through human methods but through God's. And that means we should never underestimate the power of a simple song that is sung in His name.

Big Little Jesus Songs

The Bible tells us to give to God the sacrifice of praise that is the fruit of our lips (Heb. 13:15). But were you aware that this kind of worship experience is unique to the Christian faith? No other religion sings worship to their "leader" in the same way that Christians do. People of other faiths may chant. They may recite their prayers, but they don't clap, sing, and express adoration and praise the way Christians always have.

And why is this? We Christians actually have something wonderful to sing about. And we know that we have an actual Person to receive our praises.

I distinctly remember the first time I watched Christians worship. Before I became a Christian, I went to a high school Bible study. I didn't actually attend it, but I sat at a distance, where I could hear these teenagers singing what I thought were these silly little Jesus songs. I don't remember if anyone had a guitar. As they sang, I thought, *This is very strange. They are sitting on the front lawn of a high school campus singing songs about God. These guys are clearly mentally disturbed. I really feel sorry for them. Look at them!*

But over time, as I continued to watch and listen, it became clear to me that there was something very real and profound going on. It wasn't just that I could tell that these people really believed what they were singing. I could sense that Someone was really on the receiving end of their praise. They were clearly not just singing but communicating.

And it was actually this—observing the true worship of Christians—that made me aware that there was a God and that I didn't know Him.

Remember when Paul and Silas began to praise God in jail? They had been arrested for preaching the gospel. Their backs had been ripped open with a Roman whip, their feet fastened in metal stocks and pulled as far apart as possible, causing excruciating pain. They were then thrown into a dark, cavelike hole filled with filth and stench. They could have become angry at God, but instead we read that they sang and rejoiced: "Around midnight, Paul and

> *I* COULD TELL THAT THESE PEOPLE BELIEVED WHAT THEY WERE SINGING. BUT, MORE THAN THAT, I SENSED THAT SOMEONE WAS ON THE RECEIVING END OF THEIR PRAISE.

Silas were praying and singing hymns to God, and the other prisoners were listening" (Acts 16:25, NLT). Instead of groans, songs issued from their mouths. Instead of cursing the men who had them arrested, they blessed God. Instead of complaining or calling on God to judge those who had inflicted their pain, Paul and Silas prayed. No wonder the other prisoners were listening to them.

When an earthquake shook the walls, the first thing the Philippian jailer said was, "What must I do to be saved?" It was obvious to him that Paul and Silas had been having a very real encounter with a very real God. Through worship the jailer had witnessed an intimate relationship between God and man in action, and it opened his heart to the truth of the gospel.

Compare what God accomplished through the apostle Paul's songs in a moldy cell to what Paul of the Beatles' songs accomplished!

Sometimes prior to a stadium crusade people have asked me, "Why do you have worship at these things? Many of the people coming aren't Christians anyway. They probably don't even know the songs. Why don't you just have performers or choirs sing?"

My answer is simple. When unbelievers find themselves surrounded by literally thousands of people truly worshiping God, immediately they say, "What is going on here?" They're aware that we're not just standing around singing songs, lighting Bics, or crooning the national anthem at a baseball game. We are singing to the Lord. And He is inhabiting the praises of His people.

Lessons from the Well

One of the key passages of Scripture on worship is found in a simple conversation Jesus had at a well with a woman who'd been married five times. We pick the conversation up in John chapter 4:

The woman said to Him, ". . . Our fathers worshiped on this mountain, and you Jews say that in Jerusalem is the place where one ought to worship." Jesus said to her, "Woman, believe Me, the hour is coming when you will neither on this mountain, nor in Jerusalem, worship the Father. You worship what you do not know; we know what we worship, for salvation is of the Jews. But the hour is coming, and now is, when the true worshipers will worship the Father in spirit and truth; for the Father is seeking such to worship Him. God is Spirit, and those who worship Him must worship in spirit and truth."
John 4:19-24, NKJV

What does it mean to worship in spirit and in truth? It simply means that we are to worship rightly with both our mind and our heart. You worship in truth when you worship the one true God and when you know who you're worshiping and why.

When we worship in truth, we are agreeing with God about who He is, what He can do and has done, and what He is asking of us. Then we respond by telling Him so. "Yes, Lord, You are very great. Yes, God, You are awesome, and I love You. I praise You and honor You for who You are and what You have done. I lift up Your name right now!"

*W*ORSHIP IS GOING TO BE MORE EFFECTIVE WHEN IT IS BASED ON AN ACCURATE UNDERSTANDING OF WHO GOD IS.

This is why Bible study and worship go hand in hand and are both crucial to the church. Worship is going to be more effective when it is based on an accurate understanding of who God is. So as we learn more about His nature, His character, His plans, and His purposes, then our worship is in truth—a response to what we know is true about God.

Colossians 3:16 puts it all together and says, "Let the word of Christ dwell in you richly as you teach and admonish one another with all wisdom, and as you sing psalms, hymns and spiritual songs with gratitude in your hearts to God" (NIV). Notice the elements: teaching and worship. This is worshiping in truth, and it's why only a Christian is capable of truly worshiping God.

The second half of the equation, which the Word actually lists first, is worshiping in spirit. Our worship of God should engage the mind, but it should also engage the affections, the heart, and our emotions and spirit. That does not mean that worship has to necessarily be emotional or involve an outward emotional display to be "in spirit." But it does mean it can be.

If we see someone get excited at a football game and throw his hands in the air to cheer for his favorite player, we think nothing of it. But if someone comes to church and lifts his hands in reverence to the Creator of the universe, some will say, "Look at that fanatic!"

There is nothing wrong with expressing ourselves emotionally as we respond to our awesome God. In fact, the word *worship* comes from an old English word that could be translated "worth-ship." In other words, we praise and honor a God who is worth it, who deserves our praise. We are told in Revelation 5:12 that in heaven there is a loud voice saying, "Worthy is the Lamb, who was slain, to receive power and wealth and wisdom and strength and honor and glory and praise!" (NIV).

When God says, "worship in spirit and in truth," He's saying that we should above all worship sincerely. God doesn't want us to fake it with Him but to be honest in our worship. David had more problems than most people, and he poured them out even as he worshiped the Lord continually in his psalms. As a result of his worshiping with his spirit, again and again we see him come back to his senses about God's love for him.

The Pharisees thought they were experts on worship. They would even stand on the street corners and make sure that everyone knew they were worshiping. They would sound a trumpet and give their great gifts. They would recite their long prayers. But Jesus said, "Let me tell you something about these guys. You think they're true worshipers. But the truth is, they draw near to me with their mouth, but their hearts are far from me" (see Mark 7:6-7).

So we see that it is possible to appear to worship God but not be doing so in spirit and in truth.

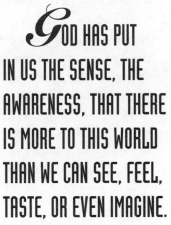

Let's face it. The kind of praise that will change the world won't happen when people are dutifully singing out of a hymnal. We all have had times when we realize that we're just going through the motions. We're singing a song, not lifting our voice to our Savior. Or we're clapping and laughing without a thought for what we're actually celebrating.

GOD HAS PUT IN US THE SENSE, THE AWARENESS, THAT THERE IS MORE TO THIS WORLD THAN WE CAN SEE, FEEL, TASTE, OR EVEN IMAGINE.

God wants us to engage in worship with intelligence as well as emotion as we learn to worship "in spirit and in truth."

Upside-Down Principles of Worship

The ability to worship is one of the distinguishing marks of humans as compared with animals. My dog doesn't sit in his backyard and lift his paws to the Lord and bark out his praises. Yes, he barks sometimes, but I guarantee he is not contemplating the wonders of eternity. He's probably thinking about food or strangers passing by.

In contrast, God has placed eternity in the human heart. That simply means that God has put in us the sense, the awareness, that there is more to this world than we can see, feel, taste, or even imagine.

A number of words are translated "worship" in the Bible. The one used most frequently, *shachah,* means to bow down and do homage. Unlike animals, human beings have a drive to bow down to something. To pay homage to something. To offer reverence and respect for God.

But we have something else animals don't have—pride. And so God asks us to do what we were uniquely created to do but what our sinful nature rebels against. In fact, many aspects of worship go against our natural tendencies. Worship is a spiritual act with spiritual consequences. And if we're not living upside down, if we're operating on the world's principles, then worship probably doesn't make much sense to us.

So what kind of praise is powerful, upside-down praise? And what kind of people offer it? When we look in the Scriptures, we see four key qualities of those people who changed the world through their upside-down praise of God.

1. They lavishly and extravagantly praised a God who needs nothing.

Why does a God who has everything and needs nothing want us to worship Him?

A lot of people stumble over this. Our tendency is to praise people whom we think need it and who we believe look up to us and our opinion. We may praise a friend's golf swing as much for his sake as for any other reason. As a result, we can easily get stingy with God without even realizing it. *God doesn't need me to boost His ego!*

That's true. God may not need our worship, but He desires it. He wants a tender, intimate relationship with us, and praise is one way we express our affection. In fact, another word that is used for worship in the Bible is one that literally means to "kiss toward." So putting these two words together, we get a whole new idea of what intimate worship is and should be.

The Bible tells us in Psalm 63:3, "Because Your lovingkindness is better than life, my lips shall praise You" (NKJV).

That means that we need to verbally communicate our affection. A wife can feel that her husband doesn't love her because he never says it. Or we may know that our spouse loves us, but we still want to hear him or her say, "I love you. I appreciate you. I'm so glad you're in my life."

God knows that worship costs us something—time, concentration, and, sometimes, real effort. But that's also when our gift of affection or affirmation can mean the most to us—-and to Him.

Mary was an upside-down woman in the Bible. One time Jesus was in the home of Mary and her sister, Martha (see John 12). The Bible says that Mary got out a box of expensive ointment (some say it was worth an entire year's wages), broke it and anointed Jesus with it. The fragrance filled the room. She wiped His feet with her hair and tears.

Mary wanted to give Jesus something that was valuable and precious to her. So with complete abandon she poured a year's wages over his feet. But she didn't care about that. She was saying with these actions, "Lord, I want to show you in a tangible way my commitment to you."

In a similar way, when David bought a field from Ornan that he wanted to use for his worship of God, Ornan said, "You're the king. This is for the Lord. Take it." But David understood worship. He said, "I'm not going to give to the Lord that which costs me nothing. I will pay top dollar" (see 1 Chron. 21:24).

2. They worshiped the Lord even when they didn't feel like it.
An upside-down believer goes against his tendency to say, "Oh man. I have a cold. The car is not working properly. I'm not in the mood to worship today, so I won't."

Think about Job. In a matter of hours he lost his family, his possessions, and his health. Everything fell apart. And when it was all said and done, what did Job do? Curse God? No. The

Bible says he fell down and worshiped. He said, "Naked I came from my mother's womb, and naked shall I return there. The Lord gave, and the Lord has taken away; blessed be the name of the Lord" (Job 1:21, NKJV).

I worship God because He deserves my praise—not because I feel like it. That's important. You should worship Him because He is always worthy of your praise whether things are going badly or well. This doesn't mean that you worship and thank Him for the bad things. It means you give thanks in the midst of difficult circumstances. We're not required to give thanks for bad things like car wrecks and broken arms.

Ultimately we give thanks for the fact that God is still on the throne—no matter how bad things get. The Bible says, "Rejoice in the Lord always" (Phil. 4:4, NKJV). And when we praise God in spite of difficult circumstances, that's when non-Christians will listen to what we have to say.

Anybody can sing when things are going well. But when the bottom drops out, when hardship hits and you keep singing, that's something unique to the Christian—and it startles the world.

Back to the story of Paul and Silas in prison. After they've sung praises to God, there is a mighty earthquake. With the walls down, the other prisoners are free to escape. Realizing that the prisoners under his guard are escaping, the Philippian jailer prepares to commit suicide rather than face the penalty from his own superiors.

Suddenly, to his surprise, Paul shouts out, "Don't do yourself any harm—we are all still here!"

And do you know what the next words out of the jailer's mouth were? "Sirs, what must I do to be saved?" (He's certainly changed his tune—"Sirs"!)

The jailer is moved and deeply impressed by the faith of Paul and Silas—which has enabled them to worship God in such miserable circumstances and in such great pain. And they haven't escaped, even when they could have. All of this opens the jailer's heart to the message of the gospel (see Acts 16:25-33).

3. They wouldn't bow down to idols.
We were all created to worship. And everybody on the face of the earth *does* worship. We don't all worship the God of heaven. But we all worship someone or something. If you are not worshiping the true and living God, you will worship a god of your own making or some false god.

It may be a sports figure. It may be an actor or a musician. It may be your own body. But everybody bows at some kind of altar. Everyone, everywhere, worships. It's the fundamental drive of life. Even atheists, skeptics, Republicans, and Democrats worship. Insurance agents and lawyers worship. Because that is one of those unique distinctions of humanity.

The story is told of a Japanese warlord who was known as Hitioshi in the late 1500s. He decided that he wanted a colossal statue of Buddha created to put in a temple in Kyoto, Japan. So he got fifty thousand workers, who worked on it for five solid years—around the clock. They had just completed this colossal Buddhist statue and erected it in the temple, when the earthquake of 1596 struck. It brought the roof down on the shrine and ruined the statue. In a rage, Hitioshi fired an arrow at the fallen Buddha and yelled out, "I put you here at great expense, and you can't even look after your own temple."

Ultimately we give thanks for the fact that God is still on the throne—no matter how bad things get.

That's the problem with a false god. It can't hear you or see you. It's not even aware of you because it's not real.

But the true God, the living God, can not only take care of a temple; He can also take care of you.

4. They worshiped with their whole life.

Worship is not only what we do when we lift our hands or our voice. It's the way we live. We worship the Lord, or don't, through our life. We worship or not through the way we do our job. We worship or not through the way we give.

True worship is the living of our life in a way that is pleasing to God. Our singing and our prayer are only the outward manifestations of a life lived for the glory of God.

Hebrews 13:15-16 provides a good overview of what worship ought to be. "Through Jesus, therefore, let us continually offer to God a sacrifice of praise—the fruit of lips that confess his name. And do not forget to do good and to share with others, for with such sacrifices God is pleased" (NIV).

We can worship God just as much through the giving of our time and resources as we do through raising our hands and singing. Paul thanked the believers for the gift they had sent to him through a man named Epaphroditus. And in Philippians 4:18 Paul made this statement about this gift, showing that a gift can be an act of worship. He said, "I have received full payment and even more; I am amply supplied, now that I have received from Epaphroditus the gifts you sent. They are a fragrant offering, an acceptable sacrifice, pleasing to God" (NIV).

If you were to come to the church I pastor, Harvest Christian Fellowship, you would drive to Riverside, California, on a Sunday morning for one of our three services and pull into our parking lot. As you pulled in, someone standing out in the hot sun would direct you to a parking place. That man or woman is worshiping the Lord by giving time. If you take your children to their class, others will be waiting there to care for them. They are going to minister to your child until you return for them. They are worshiping the Lord with the gifts they have.

Then as you walked into the auditorium, an usher would welcome you, give you a bulletin, and help you find a seat. You would be led through the service by a worship team of skilled and God-honoring musicians. Then you would listen to me speak. And, we hope, all of it would be worship.

If you made a commitment to follow Christ, you would be met by a team of loving follow-up counselors, who would walk you through the basics of what it is to follow Jesus Christ.

First Corinthians 10:31 says, "Whatever you eat or drink or whatever you do, you must do all for the glory of God" (NLT).

Fullness of Joy

A final reason to worship is that it changes us. It changes our perspective on our problems, and it brings us into God's healing presence. David once wrote, "Better is one day in your courts than a thousand elsewhere" (Ps. 84:10, NIV).

But we don't worship God to *get* anything. The upside-down believer knows this. God doesn't want to be used as a means to an end. He *is* the end. He is the object of our aim. As A. W. Tozer said, "Whoever seeks God as a means toward desired ends will not find God. God will not be used."

God is looking for those who will worship in spirit and in truth. He is looking for those who are worshiping Him because He is more than worthy, who will sing their song in the night, who will worship with their whole life so that all the world will see and know that He inhabits His people's praise.

A FINAL REASON TO WORSHIP IS THAT IT CHANGES US. IT CHANGES OUR PERSPECTIVE ON OUR PROBLEMS, AND IT BRINGS US INTO GOD'S HEALING PRESENCE.

And for those who do, there's a sweet reward. When I bring pleasure to God, I find personal pleasure. "You will show me the path of life; in Your presence is fullness of joy; at Your right hand are pleasures forevermore" (Ps. 16:11, NKJV).

TO CLAP OR NOT TO CLAP

Question: Is it better to have a planned series of songs or "let the Spirit lead"? Or is this distracting? And how much singing or clapping is too much?

Answer: The Bible tells us, "Let all things be done decently and in order" (1 Cor. 14:40, NKJV).

In our church we have what we call a "worship team." This is made up of many talented musicians in our church who will spend hours together practicing and working on the songs that will be sung in our services. There is no excuse for sloppy playing or singing done in the name of "letting the Spirit lead." Scripture tells us to "Sing to Him a new song; play skillfully with a shout of joy" (Ps. 33:3, NKJV). Whatever we do should be done for the glory of God. We should work at what we do and improve in it, be it singing, playing a musical instrument, or preaching.

At the same time, we want to keep the door open for the leading of the Holy Spirit. Some of the most tender moments in worship often come after a message has been given. People want to respond to God as a result of what they have heard from His Word. There are times when I have preached, and a certain song will come to mind that really fits what has just been said. And there on the platform I whisper into the ear of our worship leader, "Let's sing this song now." Sometimes I even lead it myself.

We might only sing a single line of it that somehow expresses the prayer of our heart. One danger that must be avoided in well-crafted worship is that it turns into a performance. That group is there to facilitate and lead, not to perform. If the singers or musicians begin to play or sing in such a way that I find myself

208

watching them more than thinking about the one
I should be worshiping, then some adjustments need
to be made.

As in most things, balance is the key.

QUESTIONS PEOPLE ASK

What's it like to speak to fifty thousand people?
Is there a feeling of euphoria? Is it frightening? Is it the ultimate ego trip? For me it is really none of the above. When I walk up to speak at a crusade, I believe I have a simple objective: to proclaim a simple-yet-powerful message, the gospel. I need to stay within certain parameters to do so. In that setting I am, for all practical purposes, a delivery boy. This brings a great sense of responsibility there, for I know that people may have gotten a friend, family member, or coworker out to hear the gospel, possibly for the one time in that person's life. I don't want to bungle this. I want my message to be clear, understandable, loving, and biblical.

I don't think about the huge number of people I may be speaking to but rather about the individuals who may be present—the mother with two small children who is wondering what the purpose of life is; the businessman who may have reached many of his goals but is empty inside and can't understand why; the young teenager who has been so despondent that she has thought about or even attempted suicide; the elderly man or woman who knows eternity is getting closer. I try to speak personally to them because I know they are out there. I have received letters, E-mails, and phone calls and have had personal conversations with them. I've heard their stories of conversion.

Looking back over the years, I can now plainly see that God has been preparing me for both pastoring and evangelism. I feel equally called to do both. Each brings its own joys and challenges. When I have been at home pastoring for a few months, I start getting that itch to go do some evangelism. Yet when I have been out crusading for a while, I look forward to returning home and teaching through a book of the Bible again.

Our congregation has been more than supportive of these crusades, and they pray constantly for us when we are out on the field. It is not unusual for us to take one hundred or more people from our congregation with us when we go to other cities for crusades. These people will have been trained and will go out on the streets and hand out invitations and gospel tracts, inviting people to the crusades at night. They will also help as counselors and ushers when needed. And they will pay their own way, just to have the opportunity to be used by God in this way.

We have recently done live Internet hookups so that people can join us in person during services as we have brought live updates of what God is doing. Considering the fact that we need to mobilize local churches when we come to town to do a crusade, it certainly helps, being a pastor myself, to speak to and encourage other pastors who have come on board to assist. Being a pastor of a local church also brings accountability and grounding. I plan on continuing to do both unless the Lord leads differently.

How do you balance quality and quantity?
Any pastor, teacher, and evangelist would rather speak to people than to empty seats. We all like to see growth in numbers, and we like the excitement that can generate. But my philosophy has always been to provide quality and leave the quantity up to God. I feel that if I do my best to provide the best spiritual meals I can, the people will naturally want to bring out their friends, and that has proved to be true.

We have never spent a dollar promoting our church in the community. We don't have ads in the religious section of our newspaper, nor do we try to get people to join up. Even when we were just a bunch of kids with no resources to speak of, we always tried our best to present the Lord's Word in the most contemporary and high-quality fashion possible. I don't understand it when people will let their facilities get run down—paint chipping, weeds growing, cobwebs building. Some might say, "We can't afford to keep it up!" Then get out there with a paintbrush, broom, or whatever, and do it yourself!

Having a background in graphics has always motivated me to put out printed materials that were totally contemporary. The same goes for music. So often in the church, we seem to always be a few years behind, and I think that's a shame. We certainly don't have to compromise our message in order to provide quality. I have found that many people who are not believers do not reject our message as much as the way we present it. It's not that they always are against what is in the box but rather against the paper we wrap it in.

What is your philosophy of preaching?
Preaching has been defined as truth through personality. Sometimes preachers will go too far one way or the other in this area. Technically it's impossible to provide too much truth, but it is possible to drone on and on about something that is true—until people have stopped listening. And when there's not personality in it, it's like the preacher who was asked to give a short talk before a luncheon. He had been given twenty minutes to speak, but he was going way over his allotted time. The moderator tried to get his attention, pointing to his watch, clearing his throat, but that preacher was in his own world, oblivious to the fact that people were falling asleep all around the room. The moderator tapped with his gavel, indicating that the preacher's time was up, but the preacher wouldn't stop talking. Finally, in complete frustration, the moderator threw his gavel at this long-winded preacher, missed him, and hit an elderly man who had fallen

asleep in the front row. Waking from his sleep, the old man said, "Hit me again; I can still hear him!"

I cannot think of a torment worse for me personally than listening to bad preaching. And there certainly is a lot of it around today. To me, it is almost a crime to take the living, vibrant, powerful, life-changing Word of God and deliver it in a boring way. You should be arrested for impersonating a communicator. I do believe that as teachers we should work at what we do and seek to be the most effective communicators that we possibly can be. When you find yourself cutting corners on your preparation because you think you have mastered all the skills, then stop and repent. C. H. Spurgeon once said, "I dread getting to be a mere preaching machine without my heart and soul being exercised in this solemn duty—lest it should be a mere piece of clock work." You are not a machine. Some preachers have great truths but deliver them in a thoroughly boring way. These truths should grip and move you as you express them to the people. Again to quote Spurgeon, "The Holy Spirit will move them by first moving you. If you can rest without their being saved, they will rest, too. But if you are filled with an agony for them, if you cannot bear that they should be lost, you will soon find that they are uneasy, too. I hope you will get into such a state that you will dream about your child or your hearer perishing for lack of Christ, and start up at once and begin to cry, 'O God, give me converts, or I die.' Then you will have converts."

But there is also the problem of not enough truth and far too much personality. You could also call it pulpit personality. Of course we should use our voice and body language to express the message in a compelling way. But some speakers take on an entirely different personality in the pulpit. It's almost as if they are in some kind of trance. They talk faster than they can think, they get whipped up in some kind of frenzy, or they sound as if they've come from another planet. Yet the Scripture tells us,

"The spirits of the prophets are subject to the prophets (1 Cor. 14:32, NKJV). This simply means that you can control your volume, tone, voice inflection, and—brace yourself for this one—you can control how long you speak!

Do you have any "most embarrassing moments"?
In the early years, when we were establishing our church, I was goofing around in the sanctuary with a musician friend. It was a weekday, and the church was empty. I decided to imitate a screaming preacher, and I got a bit carried away. My friend was playing furiously on the piano, and I jumped up on one of our speakers and was yelling, preacher-style, at the top of my lungs when two very conservative older ladies suddenly appeared before me. There I was, with shoulder-length hair, a full beard, jeans (bell-bottoms, of course—it was the seventies), in full crazy-preacher stance on top of a speaker.

One of the ladies said, "Excuse me, could you tell me where the pastor of this church is?" I couldn't bear the thought of admitting I was the pastor. I said, "Uh, he's upstairs in the church office." So they went to the church office and talked with my associate pastor.

I have had more than my share of faux pas and bumbling of phrases over the years. The first time I spoke in front of Chuck Smith, I was very nervous and wanted to deliver a message he would really be impressed with. I was speaking from Ephesians 6 about spiritual warfare. I intended to say, "You need to watch out for the fiery darts of the wicked one!" But what came out was, "You need to watch out for the diery farts of the wicked one!" It's hard to recover after that. That is all people will remember about your message.

One Sunday morning I was dedicating a little baby to the Lord and intended to pray, "Father, bless this little baby today." Instead I prayed, "Little Father, bless this . . ." Little Father? People started cracking up during the prayer. But I had a worse experience one day after I had just delivered a passionate evangelistic message. I was going to pray and invite people to come and receive Jesus Christ into their life. But instead of saying, "Let's pray," I said, "Let's pee!" I'm glad no one took me up on that.

Where do you find good leadership?
We have never really had any problems finding good leadership over the years at Harvest Christian Fellowship. Most of our associate pastors came to Christ in our services. They began attending and getting involved. When people want to serve the Lord at Harvest, we require that they attend for a minimum of one year first. Ironically, those who want to serve the most are the ones who are sometimes only weeks old in the faith. But they need to get a good spiritual foundation first. We have a special series of classes they must go through as well. Some have faithfully served the Lord over the years and have risen through the ranks as they have proved themselves faithful.

People may be teaching home Bible studies or helping out with counseling during the week. They begin, for all practical purposes, to function like a pastor-in-training. We identify those who have come to this point and ask them to become a part of what we call a leadership network. Our future associate pastors come from this network. It has always seemed that when an opening for another associate came up, there would be two or three in our network who were ready and raring to go.

It is really not for us to make someone a minister of the gospel. That is the work of the Holy Spirit. Our job is to identify those whom God is raising up. Look at the pattern of identifying leadership given in Acts 13:2-4:

> *While they were worshiping the Lord and fasting, the Holy Spirit said, "Set apart for me Barnabas and Saul for the work to which I have called them." So after they had fasted and prayed, they placed their hands on them and*

sent them off. The two of them, sent on their way by the Holy Spirit, went down to Seleucia and sailed from there to Cyprus. NIV

Notice that it says, "The two of them, sent on their way by the Holy Spirit." God is the one who calls to ministry. We are simply to acknowledge or ratify what God has already done. The process of ordination really means very little apart from this calling from God. It is my conviction that there are many schooled, degreed, ordained men in the pulpit today who quite frankly have never been called by God. On the other hand, there are many so-called laypeople who *are* called.

One of the advantages of finding the leadership for our church in our own ranks is that we know exactly what we are getting. The cream just seems to rise to the top. The more traditional approach with many churches is to look over the resumés of prospective pastor candidates who have just graduated from seminary. Then, after deliberating over it with the board, a decision is made and a person is hired. The problem with this is that sometimes you don't really know what you are getting until much later. And it's a lot harder to let a person go than it is to hire him. Many of our associate pastors attended our church for upwards of twelve years before they came on staff. It's a biblical—and a very practical—way to go.

How do you handle growth?

A popular approach to ministry is to build a building first and hope people will fill it. It is even thought in some circles that the facilities themselves will attract certain people. I know of a pastor who once had a thriving congregation. The Lord was blessing them, and the church was growing. He decided they needed a large facility, much larger than the one they already had. In the excitement of the planning, they decided to build in an affluent area of town where many families lived. They thought that if the church had the finest day-care facilities and programs for the whole family, they could attract those people who would in turn attend their Sunday services and handle the considerable debt they were about to commit to.

When it was all said and done, they built a huge six-thousand-seat sanctuary with escalators and marble slabs on the walls behind the pulpit. It was spacious, as nice as any upscale mall, but it had one small problem: The people did not fill it. This pastor arrived in his new oversized building with fewer people then he'd had in his other adequate building. His elders ended up asking him to leave.

I have always believed that building should take place to accommodate what God has done. When we have experienced new growth numerically, we have sought to build accordingly. I haven't always seen the growth coming. We always have new people coming in, but we also have others going out. Our growth over the years has always happened in spurts—and often at very unexpected times. It is all a mystery to me. My priority is to concentrate on the quality and leave the quantity up to God.

When a church begins to grow into what we now call a megachurch, one must adjust. There was a time when I knew most people in our congregation by name. Now it is not uncommon for someone to come up to me and say something like, "I've been going to Harvest for three years and have never met you!" Frankly, I feel a bit embarrassed when a person says this. I stand at the back door after the service and shake hands with people, just like countless other pastors on Sunday mornings. But I cannot possibly know every person in our congregation.

That is where good leadership comes in. The people are able to develop relationships with our lay leaders and associate pastors, and we're able to establish accountability. Each of our pastors at Harvest oversees a number of ministries. For instance, one associate may oversee the jail-and-prison ministry, the convalescent-home outreach, and the street-witnessing team. Another may oversee the new-convert counseling, ushers, etc. This way, when we have a staff meeting, I can talk to each one and get an overview of what is going on in the various ministries of our church. Under each of these pastors are key leaders who are over other leaders implementing their particular ministry. Then we have a team of three head pastors who oversee the others. It may sound confusing, but it all works quite well. I try not to micromanage but rather to enable and encourage the others in the calling God has put on their lives. I have been practicing this approach from the very beginning of our ministry, trying to identify the gifts of people and then turning those people loose where they can make the greatest difference.

When you take this approach, you need to know that people will fail at times. Yet if you can help them to fail forward, or learn from their mistakes, they can become a great asset to the work of the kingdom in the future. I was given a chance by a man named Chuck Smith in my early days of ministry. I want to do that for others as well. Now, as the years have passed, many of our associates have gone out and started their own churches that God is blessing. These are transferable principles because they are biblical ones.

My prayer and hope for you are that you will be actively involved in a Bible-teaching, gospel-preaching church. And that your church, operating by what this world may see as upside-down principles, will make an impact on your community. Let's do our part to turn this world upside down for Jesus Christ!

ABOUT THE AUTHOR

GREG LAURIE is senior pastor of Harvest Christian Fellowship in Riverside, California. He began his pastoral ministry at age nineteen by leading a Bible study of thirty people. Today that small group has grown into a church of some fifteen thousand.

Laurie also holds evangelistic events called Harvest Crusades around the country. Since 1990 more than 2 million people have attended, and more than 171,000 have indicated their decision to follow Jesus Christ.

From the early years of Laurie's ministry, his passion has been to preach the gospel to as many people as possible and to train and equip others to do the same. His style as a pastor and speaker is contemporary and straightforward, creating a nonthreatening environment that attracts people of all ages, particularly young people.

Laurie is also the featured speaker on an international daily radio program, *A New Beginning,* and serves as a board member of the Billy Graham Evangelistic Association. Laurie's other books include:

The God of the Second Chance: Experiencing Forgiveness
Life. Any Questions?
The Great Compromise
Every Day with Jesus
On Fire
Discipleship: Giving God Your Best

The New Believer's Growth Book
A Passion for God: The Practical Power of the Holy Spirit in Your Life
notes for the best-selling *New Believer's Bible*

Whether speaking or writing, Laurie is known for his ability to apply biblical principles to current events in a way that is relevant and easily understood by people of all ages and from all walks of life. Greg and his wife, Cathe, have two children and reside in southern California.